'*On Board* is a serious story lightly told, with numerous hints and tips along the way on how boards behave and how they should. Every board member should read it... and learn.'

Baroness Joan Bakewell, broadcaster, writer and
President of Birkbeck, University of London

'John Tusa is one of the bravest and most thoughtful public servants of a generation, and one of the people I admire most in British public life.'

Rory Stewart, author, writer and politician

'John Tusa deals with the great and seldom asked questions: why do chairs and chief executives not get on? Why do boards make the wrong appointments? What does a great board look like? His answers – based on huge experience – are vital reading for chairs and trustees everywhere. This is a book on an important subject full of insight and interest: essential reading!'

Lord Tony Hall of Birkenhead CBE, Chairman of the
National Gallery and former Director-General of the BBC

'For anyone considering joining a board, especially one in the arts, this is an excellent guide for what awaits them. It gives a clear sense of how the complex issues and relationships are handled from someone who was there, and lessons in good governance have rarely been so fluently expressed. And for those interested in many leading characters of the London arts scene over the past 20 years, this is a hugely entertaining read.'

Sir Andrew Likierman,
Professor and former Dean, London Business School

'With outstanding insight, John weaves his way elegantly through misunderstandings, personal ambition, indecision, and incompetence to illustrate with clarity, the consequences of flawed Chairmanship, board composition, mistaken beliefs, and finally the privilege and honour of being part of a Board that gets it right.'

Lady Alison Myners, Chair of Royal Academy Trust

'One of the truly great and good, John Tusa has led many of Britain's cultural institutions and led them brilliantly. This book explains, modestly but straightforwardly, how he has dealt with boards of trustees as helmsman, nanny, confessor, policeman, plotter, and Scout leader. Necessary reading for anyone involved in schools, arts organisations or other non-profits.'

Richard Sennett, Chairman of Trustees, Theatrum Mundi

'Sir John Tusa has enjoyed a career of remarkable range, breadth, variety and distinction, as a journalist, broadcaster, historian and arts administrator, and also as a fully paid-up and card-carrying member of the nation's "great and good". In this timely, original and deeply important book, he recalls his experiences as a trustee and chairman of some of our foremost (and occasionally troubled) cultural institutions. *On Board* should be essential reading for anyone who cares about our nation's cultural life, and about the (good and bad) ways in which our great cultural institutions have been run and are still being run today.'

Sir David Cannadine, author, historian and Dodge
Professor of History at Princeton University

'*On Board* is an arresting and enlightening survival guide for anyone who aspires to sit on a not-for-profit board. It makes an eloquent case for the public value of the independent and good governance of our intellectual and cultural institutions – and the inherent obstacles to achieving it. This is also a riveting and, at times, excruciatingly candid account of personal learning. *On Board* charts the perilous navigation between the Scylla and Charybdis of personal rivalries and collective prevarication on which so many boards can come to grief. Anyone asked to join such a board will be well advised to learn from Tusa how codes, management theory and mission statements cannot substitute for decency, humanity and rigour, so much more difficult to achieve than to prescribe. In the end, good governance depends on good behaviour.'

Tim Gardam, Chief Executive, Nuffield Foundation, former Principal of
St Anne's College Oxford and former Chair, Ofcom Content Board

OTHER BOOKS BY JOHN TUSA

Conversations with the World
A World in Your Ear
Art Matters: Reflecting on Culture
Engaged with the Arts: Writings from the Front Line
Pain in the Arts
On Creativity: Interviews Exploring the Process
The Janus Aspect: Artists in the Twenty-First Century
Making a Noise: Getting it Right, Getting it Wrong in Life, the Arts and Broadcasting

WITH ANN TUSA

The Nuremberg Trial
The Berlin Blockade

JOHN TUSA

ON BOARD

THE INSIDER'S GUIDE TO SURVIVING LIFE IN THE BOARDROOM

BLOOMSBURY BUSINESS
LONDON • OXFORD • NEW YORK • NEW DELHI • SYDNEY

BLOOMSBURY BUSINESS
Bloomsbury Publishing Plc
50 Bedford Square, London, WC1B 3DP, UK

BLOOMSBURY, BLOOMSBURY BUSINESS and the Diana logo are trademarks
of Bloomsbury Publishing Plc

First published in Great Britain 2020

A catalogue record for this book is available from the British Library

Library of Congress Cataloguing-in-Publication data has been applied for

ISBN: HB: 978-1-4729-7599-7; eBook: 978-1-4729-7601-7

2 4 6 8 10 9 7 5 3 1

Typeset by Deanta Global Publishing Services, Chennai, India
Printed and bound in Great Britain by CPI Group (UK) Ltd, Croydon CR0 4YY

To find out more about our authors and books visit www.bloomsbury.com
and sign up for our newsletters

CONTENTS

ACKNOWLEDGEMENTS

This book could not have been written without the extraordinary cooperation of dozens of my former colleagues, with whom I served on so many boards. I am most grateful to them for their openness and candour in recalling some often-turbulent times past. I value their time in reading the chapters in which they were involved and reviewing any direct quotes attributed to them. I hope the excavation of recollections of sometimes distant battles proved to be interesting and enlightening rather than painful.

Many offered valuable and perceptive observations on my text. I was happy to incorporate most of them. The book is far better as a result. To any who may feel that their comments were disregarded, I can only offer the justification of a difference of opinion. The book might not have been written at all without some firm and friendly counselling by two former Clore Fellows, Isabel Mortimer and Emily Gottlieb. They transformed my inexplicable reluctance to start writing into a clear sense of wanting to do so – I could not be more grateful.

My work was made much easier by the speed and efficiency with which Kate Foot transcribed the great majority of the interviews.

I was supported and encouraged during the writing by Ian Hallsworth, Publisher, Bloomsbury Business, and Matt James, Assistant Editor. They have been efficiency personified.

It was a privilege to serve with so many wise chairmen, remarkable executives, capable administrators, shrewd board colleagues on several great national arts institutions. My time was immeasurably enriched by their company, their thoughts, their actions. I do not write in detail about my time on the boards of the BBC or the Barbican. Those experiences were covered in my memoir *Making a Noise*.

One person saw, observed, witnessed all of it, took part directly in some of it: my wife, Annie Tusa. Much more than a hidden hand on my shoulder, more the constant presence.

Introduction: My Long March Through the Institutions

Throughout the world, hundreds of thousands of people give their time, skills and energy to serving on a board of some sort. Many would not think of their activity in this way; many would hardly think of it at all, others as a social duty, a community act. Yet from parish councils to schools to clubs to the largest multinational corporations, the non-executive board – often carrying out a trusteeship role – plays a critical part in the ultimate success of the organization. They do not run it; they watch over it, they supervise it. The ultimate responsibility for an organization is theirs but they should not interfere in the way it is managed. This is the central paradox of the activity of 'governance'.

It is right that business schools and management theory examine how boards should work and what happens when they fail. They are usually dressed up in the overall word 'governance', a life-deadening notion, yet one that cannot be ignored.

Few such studies capture the actuality of the work and business of a non-executive board: the human interplay, the rows and rivalries, the interactive psychology of behaviour among colleagues, the costs and consequences, the career casualties of board failures, whether caused by indecision, incompetence, misunderstanding, inadvertence or just plain rivalry. A well-functioning board will enhance, or even help transform, an organization, while a badly run board can undermine the institution for which it is responsible.

For more than 30 years, I have sat on a wide range of boards. Some have been established for centuries, others have been newly created. Some have been large and unwieldy, others small and purposeful. Some have had outstanding chairs, others destructive ones. I have seen chairs and chief executives who worked in brilliant harmony and others who wrought their mutual destruction. I have tried to chair well and found it to be harder than it looks. I have seen many boards made up of dedicated members who committed large amounts of unpaid time to the institution. Others have been burdened with people who saw board membership as an opportunity for egotistic indulgence. I have sat on boards which turned an institution round from near disaster, others who were the agents of disaster. My colleagues have ranged from high-powered business people to major artists, generous philanthropists, politicians, academics and managers. Only two things have ever been certain: the unpredictability of events in the world of governance and the fact that frequently, board membership will be a time of personal learning that is painfully acquired.

These dramas are often played out in very public ways, attracting intense media coverage. When any organization, public or private, runs into difficulty over money or leadership, it becomes headline news. Heads usually roll, blame is freely scattered and righteous indignation copiously enjoyed. In these circumstances, the chances are that somewhere along the line the board responsible for the organization got things badly wrong. This is just as true in the world of not-for-profits as it is in those of business, of academe and certainly, of the arts.

It is sometimes assumed that boards in the business world are totally different from those in the not-for-profit sector. This is far less true than might first appear. Both kinds of board choose their chair and chief executive, both decide how they appoint colleagues, how they sell to or serve their public, their customers or their audience; both deal with and manage risk; both must earn money; both are responsible for image, brand, communication and reputation; both supervise the internal health of the organization. Of course, one deals with profit, the other does not. But while 'not-for-profits' are not businesses, they must be 'business-like' in the ways they manage their resources.

Whatever kind of board they serve on, members seem united in a certain bewilderment about what 'being a board member' actually involves. Too often, 'going on a board' is seen as an honorific, a mark of a person's public achievements, a pleasant life landmark. It is virtually an award – the grander the board, the greater the honour. In practice, sitting on a board, let alone chairing one, is one of the most demanding, complex and taxing activities in the world of public life. This is still not well understood. Why? What are the demands placed on boards and board members? Are they not clearly understood? Why do so many make such mistakes and why do we not do better?

This book is an account of my personal practical experiences of serving on some of the largest organizations in cultural life. It addresses many of the issues that boards I have sat on and board members I have worked with have encountered. I draw on experience from British, American and European boards, from colleagues who were lawyers, bankers, artists, businesspeople, writers, academics, musicians and administrators. No board I sat on was made up of stupid people, yet almost everyone made at least one significant mistake. With the candid reflections of many of my fellow board colleagues, I tell the story of those errors as a way of teasing out a series of lessons and practical observations that may assist others in carrying out better board practices, even avoiding errors already made. I also chart the revolution that has occurred in how boards are chosen and run themselves and the benefits that flow from such a transformation.

Some insights may come as a surprise. For example, that there is no difference between governance on a corporate board and an arts board; that businesspeople are the first to recognize that arts organizations and arts boards are extremely complex and difficult; that complying with legal obligations alone does not make for effective governance; that human psychology is more valuable for effective governance than management theory.

Serving on a board is a responsibility and a privilege. The high points are very high, the low points properly chastening. For life on a board tussles with a central dilemma, a contradiction, even: you are responsible but you have no power. If that is inconvenient or just too difficult, don't join in the first place. But you will never discover what you have missed, you will always miss what you would have learned – and that will be your loss.

1

The National Portrait Gallery: The Trustees' Rebellion (1988–2000)

Interviews with

Sir Jeremy Dixon, Dixon Jones architects

Sir Max Hastings, Trustee; former Editor-in-Chief, *Daily Telegraph*

Sir Henry Keswick, former Chairman, Jardine Matheson; former Chairman, National Portrait Gallery

Neil MacGregor, former Director, National Gallery; former Director, British Museum

Malcolm Rogers, former Deputy Director, National Portrait Gallery; former director, Museum of Fine Arts Boston, Massachusetts

Sir Charles Saumarez Smith, former Director, National Portrait Gallery

Sir David Scholey, former Chairman, UBS; Trustee and Chairman

Sir Roy Strong, former Director, National Portrait Gallery

Claire Tomalin, biographer; Trustee

This is the story of how a small group of trustees resisted huge pressure and turned around the appointment of a new director of the gallery. The intervention was only possible because the nature and membership of the board of trustees had recently been significantly changed. This is also the story of the transformation of a venerable national institution into a modern, open-minded, professional, efficient, stylish, adventurous centre of the arts. It did so as the political environment in which museums and galleries in the United Kingdom existed began to change. Modernization of governance was at the heart of what I witnessed at the National Portrait Gallery (NPG), though the word was hardly used at the time and barely understood.

Located just north of Trafalgar Square in a handsome Italianate palace built by Ewan Christian (1814–95) and completed in 1896, the institution was at the receiving end of what became later known as the 'Whitehall Managerial Revolution' of the 1980s. No arts organization was untouched by its principles. To its credit, the Gallery adapted to the new environment and took its opportunities with commendable speed.

For many in London, the NPG, with its discreet entrance, modest front door, its self-effacing façade looking northwards, turned away from Trafalgar Square, sitting alongside the palatial splendour of the National Gallery, was often mistaken for a branch of its grander neighbour, or a side entrance perhaps. Its subject matter was a problem. Portraits – did anyone take them seriously now? And British ones too, how parochial was that? How could it even rub shoulders with the glittering rooms of several centuries of European masterworks next door? It was at best a place of curiosity, national, antiquarian curiosity, much-loved by the select few who chose to love it.

The NPG had its particular raison d'être, a decent and serious one; the belief that a nation should see a view of itself through the faces of those who had shaped its history. Or had been randomly selected and painted at the time. It was a 'gathering in' of people and paintings that had survived and were available. No better, no worse. Like Lord Melbourne's *mot* about the importance of the Order of the Garter, 'There is no damned merit in it', so with the old NPG. Yet no other country or nation had such a collection or much cared about 'history through likeness'. It was in every sense 'very English'. Some saw this as its strength.

Under the directorship of the English art historian Roy Strong, the NPG burst into life and into the public eye. He was just 32 when he became gallery director on 1 June 1967. In his diaries, Strong records his 'exultation. I apparently swept the Board. But the tasks ahead are terrific and daunting and exhilarating'. He knew the gallery was poorly funded, was 'a drear place, with the portraits uncleaned and glazed, hung virtually frame to frame across acres of wall space'. And the trustees who had appointed him and with whom he would have to work? 'A great institution had gone to sleep, presided over by a Board of Trustees, headed by Lord Kenyon, which was certainly conservative in spirit, not to say almost reactionary'.

Strong was 'determined to change the perception of the institution'. He started with his own image. He abandoned the safe suits and sober ties expected of a gallery director; he would be himself, 'Dr Strong of the Fedora hat and maxi-coat, the Regency jacket and ruffled shirt'. Some were shocked, others startled. More were at least jolted by his carefully cultivated clothes and appearance, his studied affectations of voice and manner: Were gallery directors supposed to look, behave, talk like this? Some, like the journalist, Quentin Crewe, saw the point, but also the latent contradictions involved: 'It is simply incredible that the Trustees of such a fuddy-duddy organization should pick a witty, mischievous man of 32 to look after the likenesses of the figures of British history.'

Strong had to succeed and succeed he did. His masterstroke was a major retrospective of '600 Cecil Beaton Portraits 1918–68' in November 1968, though then Chairman, Lord Kenyon, was appalled by what he saw as the 'modernism' of the exhibition design. People flooded in;

they queued up the Charing Cross Road to see it; national television news covered it. Strong noted with satisfaction in his diary: 'The Gallery had arrived! It is associated with the land of the living instead of being an artistic morgue.'

Almost inevitably, Strong fell afoul of the trustees. He found the chairman, Lord Kenyon, 'so conventional that he is becoming a bore'. He called one trustees' meeting 'perfectly horrible', adding that the trustees' 'ignorance appals me'. They responded in kind. Field Marshal Sir Gerald Templer, victor in the Malayan Emergency, one of the few successful counter-insurgency operations undertaken by Western powers during the Cold War, told him to 'get your hair cut'. Lord De l'Isle shouted: 'You are egocentric. Everything is you. We run the Gallery, I am watching out for you,' while Lord Euston demanded that the trustees be consulted about the decoration of galleries, down to choosing the colour of the paint. As a case study of dysfunctional governance, with a weak chairman, inappropriate trustees and a brilliant, over-powering director, it could not be bettered. Only Strong's success in mounting brilliant exhibitions saved him, as did the timely opportunity to become the youngest director at the Victoria and Albert Museum (V&A) in 1973. Job done, though he had shown what this still-shy, reclusive gallery of portraits could do. The NPG could return to a fond, public obscurity. Indeed, most still thought it was the back door to the National Gallery.

In 1988, I received an entirely unexpected phone call from John Hayes, then director of the NPG. I was two years into my position as managing director, BBC World Service at Bush House in the Strand, London. Institutionally, BBC World Service and the NPG were close neighbours. Would I consider becoming a trustee of the gallery? I observed that I knew nothing of the art and history of portraiture and it was unclear what I could contribute. Later, over coffee in his office, John Hayes explained that they wanted a trustee with experience of and contacts in the media world. I decided, selfishly, that it would be idiotic to turn down such an unexpected and attractive invitation. There was no formal interview, no request for a personal statement, no selection process. If there had been competition for the post, I knew nothing of it. Those were the old days. I note too that in 12 years as a trustee, my contributions were hardly ever on my supposed area of professional expertise – there is a lesson there!

My first board meeting of trustees in February 1989 was daunting: the distinction, the scholarship, the seniority of the other people in the portrait-lined, leather-chaired, green-lamp-shaded boardroom. This was a branch of Pall Mall clubland just across from Trafalgar Square. The English establishment in all its powerful array – social and academic – surrounded me.

The then chairman, Professor Owen Chadwick, was master of a Cambridge college, professor of modern history and author of books on Christianity. Chadwick was an ordained priest, a keen rugby player and strikingly good-looking. There was the Duke of Grafton, the 11th of his kind, 'Hugh' to his friends, descendant of King Charles II, active in preserving ancient churches and buildings. Another glance took in Sir Oliver Millar, surveyor of The Queen's Pictures for 16 years, first director of the Royal Collection, authority on Thomas Gainsborough and Anthony Van Dyck. Next to him sat Sir Lawrence Gowing, first Principal of Chelsea College of Art, then of the Slade School. No one could overlook the Marquess of Anglesey, 'Henry', whose ancestor lost a leg at the battle of Waterloo. Active in preserving historic buildings, he famously penned a seven-volume *History of British Cavalry 1816–1919*, universally greeted as a masterpiece.

At that time, 'service' on a public trustee board meant long service, usually very long. Chadwick's predecessor as chairman, Lord Kenyon, retired in 1988 after being a trustee for 35 years, and chairman for 22 of them. Hugh Grafton was a trustee for 31 years, vice-chairman for 26;

Lawrence Gowing stood down, aged 88, after 28 years on the board. Oliver Millar served for 23 years. It was another time, another world.

And this was quite a board, devoted to and knowledgeable about the most rigorous parts of art history. Scholarly beyond question, authoritative on most aspects of the Gallery's holdings, dedicated to the core activities of research, study, conservation, preservation and discovery that would keep the collections for posterity. If they were prepared to give their time and knowledge to the NPG for decades, who could fault them?

Not that they were active or interventionist in the way sometimes expected of modern boards. Deputy Director Malcolm Rogers noted that John Hayes, the director, 'ran the show' alongside Owen Chadwick, his chairman. In fact, Hayes saw the trustees, distinguished as they were, as rather 'a nuisance'. They got in the way.

For a total newcomer to this world, it was an immense privilege to share the room with such people. Awesome too. These men – all men – were deeply serious, unfailingly polite, always thorough. They were rather glorious. But their world in the gallery scene was about to change, totally, dramatically, irrevocably and for the better.

It was as if Whitehall had decided that this excellent but antique world of scholars and historians had had its day. Trustees began to be required to take on a greatly increased range of tasks. An unheralded, quiet administrative revolution occurred. From 1988, the NPG was given responsibility for its entire estate, buildings, property instead of relying on the remote and unreliable hand of a government department, the Property Services Agency (PSA). In 1992, the Gallery would become an incorporated body under the Museums and Galleries Act, allowed to and expected to earn money through commercial activities. These were big steps towards managerial independence.

This expansion of gallery responsibilities was accompanied by a radical reform of the trustee system. Terms of five years, probably renewable, were to be the norm. Those appointed under this system would reflect the changed landscape involved in running a gallery. I became a trustee in November 1988 at the same time as two others: the sculptor, Eduardo Paolozzi, and the publisher, George Weidenfeld. Whatever we were, none of us was a scholar or outright academic authority. In retrospect, we may have been chosen because we had expertise in our own fields and were very practical people. We joined a board which already contained businessmen such as Henry Keswick and Marcus Sieff, the journalist Susan Crosland and historian Margaret Gowing. Perhaps we tipped the balance; with our arrival, the tone of the trustees could seriously change without being lowered.

In any case, the NPG was already spreading its wings. In 1989, a £12 million Development Plan was launched. All administration and offices would be moved across the adjacent street, Orange Street, into a newly renovated building. This allowed the whole length of the ground floor of the main building to become galleries for the very first time. The appeal got a massive boost from a £2 million donation from the philanthropist, Drue Heinz, for the archive and library. For her, the NPG was something of a pet project. Some believed that she 'was in love' with Owen Chadwick, or at least with his chiselled profile. Later, her generous instincts but somewhat proprietary feelings for the Gallery may have led to her overplaying her hand.

The 1989 Development Plan suggests an organization with significant ambitions. The evolving board under Owen Chadwick's chairmanship began to find its voice. Sometimes referred to as 'saintly', Chadwick was a subtle and consummate politician. No one could write church history without picking up some of the historical tricks of argument, persuasion and manipulation. As a later colleague described him: 'He was a great cleric, an incredibly worldly cleric, who managed in a holy way to do exactly what he wanted to do.'

In late 1988, the art world was abuzz with speculation as to where the fabulous Thyssen-Bornemisza collection of art would find a home. Some believed its destination should be London. Oddly for a specialist portrait collection, the NPG was identified by some as a likely 'good home' for what was a treasure trove of non-portrait paintings. For good measure, it might 'take over' the potentially vacant Somerset House. Such ignorant ideas could be dismissed easily enough as unfunded, unfundable and wholly impracticable. They suggested a prevailing ignorance about what the NPG really did.

Then it became political. Margaret Thatcher saw the acquisition of the Thyssen paintings as a potential jewel in her artistic crown. Whitehall officials briefed that the Prime Minister 'wanted it'; London, they wheedled, deserved the Thyssen collection. More directly, they advised NPG managers that they 'shouldn't go against Thatcher.' More specifically still, they added: 'Don't attack her for it, support her.'

The trustees were not beguiled by Whitehall's siren voices nor fooled by its weasel words, they stood firm. They knew the Gallery had neither the skills nor resources, still less the inclination, to embark on such a risky adventure, to embrace a collection so distant from its own holdings and purposes. The Thyssen collection later found its handsome resting place in Madrid whereupon the trustees were vindicated in their caution and common sense.

Politics would not go away. In February 1989, a letter arrived with a still more dramatic proposal: why couldn't the NPG move from its 'dingy' premises off Trafalgar Square and throw in its lot with the shiny, new, emerging (if then troubled) Canary Wharf? The developer, Paul Reichmann, offered the NPG a brand-new building there at an all-up cost of £37 million.

The trustees considered the specifics of Reichmann's letter at a board meeting a week later. It made revealing reading: the developer calculated his offer to the NPG as amounting to £11.8 million. This consisted of a 'free site' said to be worth £4 million, half the infrastructure costs (unspecified) of £2.5 million, a 'contribution' to construction costs of £2.5 million and (unspecified) savings on construction materials of 10 per cent. The letter went on. If the existing historic premises were sold for, say, £13.5 million, the NPG only – 'only'! – had to raise £15 million to get a glossy new building in what he called the 'coming' part of London for an overall cost of £37 million.

The letter made no mention of running costs at the new building in Canary Wharf, no business plan, no consideration of the impact on visitor numbers. But Canary Wharf was a high government priority, a political initiative. Should the trustees not take this into account? The Hong Kong businessman, Henry Keswick, and the Duke of Grafton, a pleasantly unusual coupling, wanted the offer rejected out of hand. Other trustees, marshalled by Owen Chadwick, decided that the director, John Hayes, should at least continue to explore options but without commitment. This was a sensible piece of procrastination.

At the next trustees' meeting in May 1989, we were advised that the total outturn cost of the new gallery at Canary Wharf had doubled to £68 million. For good measure, the Minister of the Arts advised that the existing historic building could not 'easily' be disposed of. (He might have added 'at all'!) The project, cooked up in a political attempt to persuade doubters that Canary Wharf was the place to be, an attractive environment for work and play, was dead.

This more pragmatic board of trustees had met a complex and possibly treacherous problem effectively. We declined to be rushed or influenced on political grounds; we judged that abandoning the so-called 'processional route' through Central London would savage visitor numbers. We had seen through the smoke and mirrors of some very speculative numbers. It was time to concentrate on our own vastly preferred 'Plan B', the Main

Building and Orange Street development. The board formally gave the go-ahead in November 1989.

One further 'political' decision faced the trustees. As the NPG stood side by side, back to back with the National Gallery, some practical cooperation seemed sensible, desirable even. The possibility of a 'ground link' connection was raised, allowing visitors at one gallery to move to the other without leaving the premises and going out onto the street. Whatever we thought about it, a marginal improvement to visitor circulation at best, our neighbour's trustees turned it down flat because of possible over-crowding at the National Gallery's cafes. Besides, the two institutions had a poor record of cooperation in the past. Unknown to all of us, a far more ambitious plan of cooperation was soon to appear.

The summer of 1992 witnessed the final changing of the 'old guard' among the trustees. The Duke of Grafton and Sir Lawrence Gowing both stood down after decades of service. A board minute thanking them for their service noted Gowing had 'delighted his colleagues with his wit and unpredictability'. Both deserved thanks and respect for their skills and dedication. The incoming trustees confirmed the arrival of the modern era of governance: the diplomat Sir Antony Acland, banker Sir David Scholey, biographer Claire Tomalin and social worker Winifred Tumim. This new board was to make an historic decision about the NPG's future direction within the year.

Director John Hayes, assisted by his deputy, Malcolm Rogers, and a head of administration, John Wykeham, successfully pressed ahead with the Orange Street development, on time and on cost. With this under control, in May 1993, Hayes announced his intention to retire on 21 January 1994. The trustees would face the single biggest responsibility and challenge that any board has to deal with: appointing a chief executive.

In the 1980s, with museums and galleries firmly part of the Civil Service in questions of staffing, posts such as the Director of the National Portrait

Gallery were handled by the Civil Service Commission. The process started simply and conventionally enough. There were two strong internal candidates: the Deputy Director, Malcolm Rogers and the Keeper of 20th Century Portraits, Robin Gibson. Rogers was highly capable, an expert on and collector of portraits, who had been an effective leader on fundraising and the capital project. Some said John Hayes was lucky to have him managing the strategic decisions. Gibson was a gentler character, highly expert, easy to underestimate, much-loved by staff. From the start, Rogers looked the likely successor.

Then a third candidate appeared, the outsider, Charles Saumarez Smith from the V&A. In Civil Service terms, he was on the right grade and thought personally that promotion to a directorship should not be out of the question. During the summer, a preliminary interview was held at the Civil Service Commission with eight trustees present – I was not one of them. According to Claire Tomalin, after a gruelling six-hour session without a break, the Civil Service representative ruled that the final shortlist of two could not be made up of internal candidates alone. Robin Gibson would be dropped, leaving the trustees to choose between the insider, Malcolm Rogers, and the outsider, Charles Saumarez Smith.

The trustees rebelled at this apparent restriction on their right to choose the director. They would not be bullied by ancient Civil Service practices. When Claire Tomalin wrote to me on 23 September 1993, she reminded me that I had previously stated that the appointment of the director was the most important decision the trustees had to take. It could not therefore, she argued, be circumscribed by Civil Service shibboleths. Robin Gibson had given a persuasive first interview and should be seen by the full board of trustees. I agreed.

The next day, I wrote to Owen Chadwick arguing that 'the Trustees should be presented with a real choice; there should be a short list of three from which the Trustees should be absolutely free to choose.' I added: 'I would regard a "board of two" as not constituting a proper choice. It is a matter for the Trustees to choose how many candidates we see – we cannot be told by others how to conduct our business.' No doubt others spoke in similar terms. The matter was conceded. The full board of trustees would see Rogers, Gibson and Saumarez Smith on Monday, 4 October.

I have always deeply regretted that I could not attend such a crucial meeting. In one of the worst diary clashes of my career, I had to chair a crisis meeting of Wolfson College Council in Cambridge, where my own position was at stake. It was unavoidable in every sense. I missed one of the great board meetings, where trustees acted with robust and courageous independence.

If any observer were to rely on the official NPG Board Minute of that meeting, they would assume that the decision was despatched in a calm, cool, uncontroversial manner. Charles Saumarez Smith, it was noted, was asked what he could contribute to the Gallery and what he would change. Malcolm Rogers was questioned about his vision and if he wanted to change anything in particular. Robin Gibson was asked about his presentation of the collection and the exhibition programme. No doubt the actual questioning was both more varied and more rigorous. Trustees then gave their 'personal opinion' about each candidate – details unrecorded. The Minute ends: 'Finally, a vote was taken and the Trustees decided by a majority to recommend to the Prime Minister the approval of Charles Saumarez Smith as the new Director.' Simple. It confirmed the Whitehall dictum that 'Minutes of meetings are designed to conceal rather than reveal'.

Seldom can an official Minute have been more utterly misleading. The selection board was filled with turmoil, drama and a walk out. The lead-up had been filled with assumptions, lobbying and gossip. Many, perhaps most, expected Malcolm Rogers to get the job. He was thorough, efficient, scholarly and knew the NPG inside out. Why bother to look elsewhere? Less helpfully for him, London art world gossip was assured that 'Rogers would get it.' After all, Sir Oliver Millar, surveyor of The Queen's Pictures, was telling all and sundry that 'Malcolm was his man' and should and would become director. Millar even told the *Sunday Times* as much ahead of the selection board. Drue Heinz, the Gallery's most generous benefactor, was also known to be backing Rogers. Even wily Owen Chadwick told a trustee that while, of course, it was up to the board to decide, 'I want Malcolm.' This was not new-style governance but attempted old-style fixing. Old habits and instincts died hard.

Other trustees heard the gossip and noticed. They did not like being taken for granted, feeling rail-roaded. Claire Tomalin in particular regarded the interference of Drue Heinz, a benefactor, as just 'outrageous'. Still, the selection meeting in the afternoon of Monday, 4 October 1993 began with the presumption that Malcolm Rogers would become director. For his backers, such as Oliver Millar, Saumarez Smith was the man to stop.

Millar's first question, as Saumarez Smith recalls, was designed to be the killer: 'Young man, what exactly do you collect?' 'Portraits', of course, he meant. 'Nothing' was the honest reply or at least nothing that might stand comparison with Malcolm Rogers' considerable personal collection. It was not, however, a helpful start, though probably too blatantly barbed to have had its full effect. It was not until the banker, Sir David Scholey, asked a more open-minded question that Saumarez Smith began to feel he might still be in play as a contender.

Still, when the final discussion among trustees began, the mood, strongly influenced by Oliver Millar's personal advocacy, was in favour of Rogers. One by one, the trustees spoke up in his favour. The tide of opinion was crucially checked by David Scholey. 'If I owned the gallery,' he mused as a businessman, 'who would I choose? I would choose Charles.' He was intelligent, Scholey explained, he was an outsider and he would bring different ideas about the future of the organization into play.

Claire Tomalin spoke next. She was a newcomer and she felt new, detached from other trustees, whom no one had bothered to introduce. Feeling an outsider, she knew she should speak her mind; what was the point of being on the board if she didn't? Malcolm Rogers was very good, she noted, but he had worked only at the NPG. It needed, she recalled, 'an outsider, a very qualified one, to stir things up.' Tomalin had spoken to no one else beforehand but thought it 'important to say what I did'. She backed Charles.

It might have remained a solitary protest but the next voice was that of another newcomer, Winifred Tumim. Direct and outspoken as always, she would choose Saumarez Smith. Owen Chadwick looked nonplussed at this sudden of change of mood. 'Anybody else?' he asked. When Henry Keswick, chairman designate, said, 'I could work with either,' the atmosphere changed in Charles' favour. It felt almost like the shift of opinion in the film, *Twelve Angry Men*. Chadwick picked up on the change of mood so quickly that he was soon asking, 'Can it be unanimous?' To this day, Scholey doesn't understand why Chadwick allowed the trustees to swing behind Charles without further debate. Why didn't he argue the case? What was in the mind of that subtle cleric? In any case, his appeal for unanimity was too late for Oliver Millar, who stormed out of the meeting, muttering loudly, according to Scholey, 'It was those bloody women!' Tomalin thought he behaved 'disgracefully'. Within a year or two, however, they had made their peace and Millar helped Tomalin with access to material in the Royal Collection. Other wounds were slower to heal; Millar did not speak to Scholey for a decade.

It is hard to find or feel any sympathy for what can only be described as Oliver Millar's overweening sense of entitlement. His conduct after walking out did him and Malcolm Rogers no favours. Threatening to resign (he didn't), he said 'devastation was an understatement' and demanded the British government should intervene, enlisting his cohorts of supportive London art dealers to his side. One called on Charles Saumarez Smith to withdraw, another railed at the 'supreme folly of the Trustees'. Insulated from the incestuous London art world, the *Evening Standard* lauded the trustees' 'tremendous energy and concern for fresh blood'. Seemingly, Millar never paused to think that Malcolm Rogers' unblemished reputation might be harmed by such a public display of his personal egotism.

The story has not one but two happy endings. Deeply disappointed as he must have been, Malcolm Rogers was, he recalled, 'upset for a week'. He was particularly irritated when it transpired that the great operatic diva, Dame Joan Sutherland, had been enlisted to write to then Prime Minister Margaret Thatcher about the appointment. With a week gone by, Rogers asked himself whether or not he wanted to be a gallery director. Deciding he did, he began filling in application forms without delay. It was a problematic time for such a decision. *The New York Times* had just reported no fewer than 23 museums in the United States were seeking new directors. The implication was why should anyone want to take on such a multi-tasking job? Wasn't it too difficult?

Rogers' very first attempt was undoubtedly ambitious – Director of the Museum of Fine Arts (MFA) in Boston, Massachusetts, a huge, rich, prestigious, institution. He reckoned that if he was even shortlisted, this would be a useful calling card for further application attempts. However, he landed the job and made a signal success of it at every level for 21 years.

Rogers attributes his success in Boston to Margaret Thatcher and the revolution in British museum governance: 'What made my career? Mrs Thatcher's insistence that galleries should take responsibility for their buildings, their budgets and their business. They had to justify their existence as recipients of taxpayers' investment.' This gave him a sound base of practicality and management. 'I could DO the art,' he explained, 'This meant that I could do all the other things too. It made my career.' If

Rogers was part of the general learning curve of British gallery leaders, he was also rather ahead of it. As he recalls: 'Most museum directors wanted to choose the art and the exhibition programme, regarding the rest of the job as less desirable. I relished the whole range.'

The principal happy ending was of course Charles Saumarez Smith's, plucked from comparative obscurity at the V&A to a national position in the arts sector. February 1994 was the start of a new era at the NPG, with Saumarez Smith succeeding John Hayes as director and the businessman Henry Keswick succeeding the church historian and scholar Owen Chadwick as chairman. The change in culture could hardly have been more extreme. The trustees felt new too, though Sir Oliver Millar, the last of the scholarly old guard, stepped down a year later.

Continuity, of course, existed and was acknowledged. The First Development Plan had been devised, funded and delivered by the end of 1993. Annual visitor numbers increased by one third to more than a million. The self-effacing John Hayes received less credit than he deserved for instituting the annual Portrait Award for a programme of twentieth-century commissions and the startling renovation of the twentieth-century galleries. Yet, the February 1994 trustees' meeting felt like a fresh start. It began with the figure and personality of Henry Keswick.

He was in many respects an atypical choice as chairman of a major cultural institution. Rather large, round of face and figure and, as chairman of the Hong Kong conglomerate, Jardine Matheson, extremely rich. His predecessor, the 'saintly' academic Owen Chadwick, had backed him, judging that the NPG now needed clout, influence and connections, not just with money. Chadwick was right: Keswick had the first three in spades and the fourth for good measure. Yet, by his own admission, Keswick took over riddled with self-doubt. Etonian, Guards officer, moneyed, he admits to having wasted his time at Cambridge and regarded himself as 'neither an academic nor an intellectual'. In his mind, all the trustees were either one or often both. In the judgement of one trustee, the journalist and historian Max Hastings, the fact that Keswick regarded himself as 'uncultured' was 'the highest term of praise' because it allowed him to form an extremely constructive partnership with Charles Saumarez Smith, a crucial factor in any effective board.

The relationship got off to a somewhat unorthodox start. Two months after his appointment, Saumarez Smith thought it a good idea to meet his new chairman. He was duly summoned for lunch at Jardine Matheson's City offices. As he recalls it, three men in pinstripe trousers hovered with food and wine. Keswick announced breezily: 'You do know that I didn't approve of your appointment?' (Though he had finally voted for him.) Saumarez Smith replied: 'Yes, of course I know.' This very direct candour allowed the two men to form a concordat. In Saumarez Smith's words: 'The relationship was that he was older and so in charge and as the chairman, I had to defer to him. But he had an incredible number of corporate responsibilities globally so you kept close control of your chief executive. But so long as the employee was doing what was wanted, he left them to get on with the job.' Quaintly, Keswick says that he 'treated Charles like a manager' in his company. Many might have resisted and fought such a definition of 'chairmanly primacy'. Saumarez Smith's apparent readiness to play the subservient role proved both tactical and wily.

In Keswick's mind, bred no doubt by his underlying sense of insecurity, there was only one way to be chairman: you had to be seen to be in charge. 'I dominated the board,' he said. He treated the gallery just as he did his own multi-billion company. Keswick would arrive at 8.30 a.m. every Tuesday. After quizzing Charles about visitor numbers and any financials, he would walk the offices and was not unknown to lick his fingers, running them along bookshelves to check for dust. It was an old army trick. On one occasion, he was 'brutally abrasive with staff'. Keswick's manner, Charles recalls, made it clear: 'make sure you are behaving because somebody here will give you a hard time if this place isn't kept in good order'. It was 'not my style of management but it wasn't totally wrong'. Most would have regarded it as intolerable. The new director accommodated it and, of course, provided a massive counterbalance with staff internally through his own quite different approach. Chairman and director, strikingly contrasted as individuals, in outlook and in their practices, made an unlikely but highly effective team.

Keswick's great skill and virtue was his conduct of meetings. They never ran more than two and a half hours; trustees were encouraged not to 'rabbit on' though some disliked the chairman's somewhat brusque, almost autocratic manner. But it suited Max Hastings, with his strong belief that 'Trustees don't have to talk about everything. They shouldn't feel obliged to speak if they had nothing to say'. Keswick believed any board should behave speedily, sensibly and practically, just like his business. He had no time for vagueness but always allowed the entire board to have a say and had a great respect for the trustees, admiring their variety, skills, professionalism and personal achievement. None, he said, were there 'for their vanity, their money or for a sense of grandeur'. All cared for the institution, not for themselves.

Max Hastings adds that Keswick insisted that meetings should be fun! I do not recall that they were, for Henry remained to me somewhat opaque, chilly even, always correct. During his time, the Annual Report never recognized the contribution of trustees or thanked those who had done their time. Henry often lacked the 'grace notes' of personal interaction. But I admired and valued the way he ran meetings, his insistence on not wasting time and his readiness to stand up to government in the NPG's defence. Rich men don't have to toady. Chadwick had been right.

At all events, the Keswick/Saumarez Smith duo was both business-like and productive. Based on the success of the Orange Street development of 1993, the NPG adopted an even more ambitious masterplan devised by the architects Jeremy Dixon and Ed Jones. Simple, clever, ambitious and daring, it would ready the gallery for the twenty-first century and depended on one 'political' masterstroke: an agreement with the National Gallery.

In return for giving up their ancient 'right to light' for several offices overlooking a common service yard, the National Gallery would get the NPG's West Wing. This had always sat uncomfortably in the gallery's floor plan but happily abutted and connected directly with the main National Gallery building. Could the deal be pulled off, especially in view of the poor relations between the institutions of the past?

In May 1995, NPG trustees were invited to see models of the Dixon/Jones masterplan. Breathtakingly simple, it involved 'attaching' an entire five-floor unit to the gallery's south wall. A vast escalator inside would transform internal connections, carrying visitors straight up to the brilliant but comparatively unvisited Tudor galleries. And it allowed the creation of a dazzling and long-needed rooftop restaurant with views of Whitehall down to Parliament and Westminster Abbey. When Ed Jones and Jeremy Dixon first gained access to the NPG's almost entirely unvisited roof it was, recalls Jeremy Dixon, a revelation: 'The buildings we saw from this undiscovered roof related to many of the key national institutions. We came to think of this view as an extension of the idea of a National Portrait Gallery, as being itself a kind of "national portrait". But the National Gallery had to agree. 'The Deal,' as Dixon/Jones called it from the start, had an appearance of equality but was in fact very one-sided. It could be transformative for the NPG, merely a pleasant addition for its grander neighbour, so why should they play ball?

At this stage, the personalities and personal authority of two major directors became vital. Very little paperwork was involved. Saumarez Smith saw the vast potential benefits that would accrue to the NPG. He still finds himself wondering: 'How easy, straightforward and friendly it was'. For director Neil MacGregor, the National Gallery gained little but lost hardly anything. It all seemed 'extremely simple' for him too, he recalls. There was never a question of 'doing the NPG a favour'. Rather, he saw the two institutions as being 'complementary'. Both boards were, in his view, 'trustees of the public good'. The beneficiaries of each institution were the same, the public. So, who would benefit from such cooperation? Why 'the public would benefit'. End of matter. Such clarity of thought, partly legalistic but largely moral, should not be taken for granted.

All agree that 'The Deal' was sealed with 'a handshake' between the two directors. Just that. Jeremy Dixon is convinced that he saw them standing on adjoining sections of roof and shaking hands 'across the divide', as is physically possible. There is no photographic record of this moment. Neither denies that it happened like that but they don't confirm it either. Saumarez Smith reflects that important moments conjure their own images, while MacGregor says, 'If that is what Jeremy remembers, then so be it.' For both men, Dixon's retained memory, that striking image, contains its own truth and validity.

There are no grounds for disputing Dixon's judgement that the achievement of 'The Deal' reflected the huge personal authority of two powerful directors. Would anyone behave with such clarity, so decisively, in today's 'risk averse' circumstances? Would any trustee board let them?

At the very next trustees' meeting in July 1995, we were told that 'The Deal' had been done. Backed by a sizeable private donation from the financier and philanthropist Christopher Ondaatje and almost £12 million from the Heritage Lottery Fund, the Ondaatje Wing opened in May 2000 and was hailed in the annual report as the 'most significant development in the history of the institution since the opening of the original building in April 1896'.

In the meantime, the NPG, with the impact of its first development drawing in a steady million-plus visitors a year, consolidated its reputation as a place with appeal and clout. Others wanted to share in the success. Trustees travelled to Middlesbrough, where they were invited to set up an 'out-station' in partnership with the town's own plans for an art gallery. We visited Durham, where a similar invitation offered us much of a classical brutalist university building overlooking the River Wear. We rejected both – we would avoid 'imperial over-stretch'. Being in demand was welcome; it represented recognition of a decade of transformation from quiet, traditional, academic excellence to confident, purposeful, cultural effectiveness. Nothing of value was lost in the process.

For myself, my first experience of a major arts board was a kind but intense learning process. I had witnessed the transformation of the trustees from traditional scholarship to modern management; I saw trustees exert their independence and appoint a director they wanted; I saw two development plans successfully defined, funded and delivered; I noted the NPG's emergence as an organization of standing and public recognition.

Personally, my decade on the board introduced me to a world far wider than the narrow if intense preoccupations of journalists and broadcasters. Indescribably precious, it quite literally opened my eyes to people, practices and perspectives I would otherwise not have discovered.

REFLECTIONS

When I joined in 1988, the NPG was on the cusp; traditional ways of working and organization were no longer relevant. In its existing form, it was out of touch with the new world.

A new type of board member was steadily appointed, from a richer range of backgrounds and professions, with new skills, accepting a broader set of responsibilities and a more engaged role.

The board changed from being principally academic to one based on practical experience that saw the entire activity of the NPG in the round.

New trustees were not cowed by tradition nor by the chairman. They spoke out because they saw it as their duty. The institution benefited hugely as a result.

The trustees resisted government and Whitehall pressure and blandishments. They believed the NPG's interests should come first, rather than following a government line. Political pressure and politically motivated appointments should be resisted.

The trustees stepped away from seemingly attractive offers of expansion and cooperation. They had a clear sense of priorities. When a daring opportunity appeared – 'The Deal' with the National Gallery – they were quick to support it.

Trustees allowed two powerful, authoritative directors to act.

Trustees were collegiate, friendly, but never incestuously close. They seldom plotted or formed 'cabals'.

The trustees worked under two strikingly different chairmen: one clever, charming and subtly manipulative, the other opaque, inclined to the brusque, practical and arguably the more effective. The board adapted to the different approaches. Though the chairman appeared to dominate the director, trustees understood where effective power lay.

The NPG continued its path of modernization under successive chairmen and directors. There was continuity in its approach.

The commitment to excellence in NPG core activities – portraiture, ancient and modern – was never challenged or undermined.

Trustees freely gave more of their time to NPG activities than was formally asked for. All were enriched as a result.

Time spent in socialization made the board a pleasant place to work. Being a trustee was a responsibility, but above all a privilege.

Trustees were critical when a major donor tried to influence an appointment; still more critical when another major donor was made a trustee.

Donors or potential donors should not expect that their undoubted generosity will lead to a position of special influence.

The future question hanging over the NPG is existential: 'Is it a history of portraiture or a visual history of a nation's identity?' This is still being worked out.

2

My American Board: Taking Governance Seriously: The American Way (1991–1999)

Interviews with

William Dietel, Chairman, Public Radio International (PRI), Minneapolis; President, Rockefeller Brothers Fund (RBF)

Sir Clive Gillinson, Chief Executive, Carnegie Hall, New York City

Roger Hale, board member, Public Radio International (PRI); Chief Executive, Tenant Group

Malcolm Rogers, Director, Museum of Fine Arts (MFA), Boston, Massachusetts

Stephen Salyer, Chief Executive, Public Radio International (PRI); Director, Salzburg Seminars

Lawrence Wilkinson, board member, Public Radio International (PRI); governance consultant

I had no idea that my journey of discovery about boards and governance would continue after I left the National Portrait Gallery in 2000. While that had been a fascinating experience, I assumed it was almost certainly a 'one-off'. I did not seek to replicate or repeat it. I would not have known how to 'get on' the board of another institution, still less which one I might turn to. Besides, my time at the BBC World Service was both demanding and utterly engrossing. To seek extra-curricular involvements seemed unwise, undesirable and unnecessary, even if valuable learning might turn out to be a useful side benefit. (It took me a few years of sitting on the joint boards of management and governors at the BBC to realize what a profound and often disillusioning experience of governance it was.)

By the early 1990s, BBC World Service was extending its reach to audiences by whatever technical means we could. Shortwave transmission from huge, globally scattered relay stations, splendid installations of giant metal towers swagged in cables, had always been the mainstay of international broadcasting. It was increasingly supplemented by mediumwave and more local transmissions. A still more direct way of reaching listeners had appeared: the re-broadcasting of our programmes by local radio networks and stations in other countries.

In the United States, the influential National Public Radio (NPR), public service broadcasting largely supported by personal subscriptions, had cherry-picked BBC World Service reports for its news bulletins for years. This was marginally useful for our profile but hardly a strategic breakthrough to a wider American audience.

In 1983, a competitor to NPR emerged: American Public Radio (APR), based in the Twin Cities of Minneapolis/St Paul in the state of Minnesota. Initially consisting of 244 local radio stations throughout the United States, APR made entire programmes available to affiliates (15 years later, the total number of affiliates had grown to 800). In 1986, it began offering entire programmes from BBC World Service rather than news snippets. This represented a significant potential improvement to our reach into a mainstream US audience. We earned no income but it cost us nothing – with no transmitter costs, it was a cheap way to an audience that had previously been inaccessible. Five years later, I was invited to join the board of APR. From the point of view of my position at the World Service, it seemed a sensible invitation to accept. I did not imagine that I would also receive a crash course in serious, rigorous American-style board governance.

American Public Radio's location in the Midwest was key to its character and outlook. Minnesota was not California or New England, nor Los Angeles nor New York. With deep Scandinavian roots, a severe continental climate and a strong sense of public duty, the city, the state and their citizens owed nothing to anyone. The Twin Cities supported a renowned art gallery (the Walker Art Center), a theatre (the Guthrie), a concert hall and a full-time, world-class orchestra (the Minnesota Orchestra). They lived in the shadow of nowhere else. Minnesotans are not pushy but needed no permission to think for themselves.

The board of American Public Radio (APR) that I joined in 1991 reflected this confidence. National Public Radio (NPR) was an East Coast, Washington-beltway, centrally organized body. APR would be all-American, nationally-oriented, open and responsive to members. As one board member noted, it was intended as 'a democratisation of access of radio producers to audiences.' In doing so, it challenged the assumptions and practices of the long-established, somewhat institutional NPR. This suited the independent Minnesotan psyche perfectly. I soon found that the way the APR board conducted business was consistent with the place in which it was born.

In the nine years that I served on the board I tried to attend at least twice a year. We met in 10 different locations, from Santa Barbara in California to New Orleans, Louisiana, and Atlanta, Georgia, as well as Minneapolis, Minnesota, and Washington. The commitment to 'serving the Union' was not an empty one. Meetings were well organized, efficient, orderly, thorough and disciplined. No one had time to waste. Its composition was carefully planned. Approximately one third of the directors (board members) represented the radio station affiliates – after all, it was their business APR was serving. But they were in a minority. Good governance demanded that the beneficiaries of an organization should not also direct its activities, not a principle or practice that is universally accepted.

For the other two thirds of its members, the board majority, the first demand was for total independence of thought and advice. The second was for the range and variety of their skills and experience. At my first APR board meeting, I looked around at this entirely unfamiliar group of people. I learned soon enough that they came from backgrounds including the arts, philanthropy, corporate, business and the law. Jon Lovelace ran a large investment company based in California; Bruce Atwater was president of the huge General Mills group; Roger Horchow was serially successful in upmarket fashion retail (so successful that Neiman Marcus bought up his company); Roger Hale was president of a Minnesota manufacturer, Tenant. Martin Siegel was in a category of his own, a self-made businessman with a sense of humour and a streak of practical common sense, often delivered in the seemingly folksy form of 'My grandmother always used to say...' She was usually right. He became chair of the board of Lincoln Center in New York.

In the experience of the long-serving CEO of APR, Stephen Salyer, the members of this varied board had important characteristics in common: 'They were not all cut from the same cloth; none had paid for their position; none was there for ego-fulfilment, nor for personal vanity; all wanted to help to make things go better; they were also characterized by humility based on records of considerable achievement; there was mutual respect.' APR was in truth a small enterprise in a specialized area of activity. The fact that influential people of nationwide standing gave their time and advice spoke volumes for their understanding of civic duty.

The form, values and governance of the APR board reflected the personality and philosophy of its first chairman, Kenneth Dayton. He was president of the Minneapolis family firm of Target, a huge department store that later expanded into mass retail through the very first American shopping mall, Southdale, located just outside the Twin Cities. Today, the company stands second only to Walmart among American discount retailers.

The Daytons' earned wealth was matched by their public service commitment and sense of responsibility to their community. Ken and Judy Dayton were zealots in believing that a duty of philanthropy lay on those who possessed wealth, whether inherited, acquired or earned. In the late 1980s, Ken set out their Ten Principles for 'The Art of Giving'. These included, 'A good giver aims to be a good giver' because 'a good giver enjoys giving'. The Daytons believed that if someone was looking for financial support, you should at least hear what they had to say as soon as possible. The reason? 'I don't think of people asking me for money. I think of them as offering me an opportunity to do something important,' said Ken.

Dayton also believed that public corporations as well as individuals had a responsibility to give. He shocked many even in liberal Minneapolis by saying that corporations should give 'Five percent of their after-tax profits to the community'. One local business leader called him 'a communist'. Acting on these principles, Ken and Judy Dayton gave away $100 million to charities over 50 years.

Ken's other passion as a major businessman was governance, good governance and the improvement of governance in what Americans call the 'Not for Profit' sector (NfP). As chairman of APR from its inception, he led by example. A close colleague and later APR chairman for five years himself, William Dietel, former president CEO of the Rockefeller Brothers Fund (RBF) and later founder of the philanthropic advisory firm Dietel

Partners, observed Dayton close-up at work: 'He was masterful, very clear. The Board's first responsibility was to appoint a Chief Executive. Thereafter, it defined the organization's mission, reviewed it every year and renewed it every five years. Then it left the CEO to deliver the mission' which was to say 'get on with the job'. Throughout, Dayton was insistent: 'Don't interfere with the chief executive. Stand apart and look at strategy.' Separation of powers was essential here as it is in the US constitution.

Stephen Salyer was chief executive of APR for 17 years from 1988, several of them working with Ken Dayton as chairman. He recalls Dayton's definition of the relationship: 'The Chair and CEO must be separate and independent as people; and they must be a partnership.' The paradox of separation and partnership at the top of governance; both the distance and the closeness were essential.

Dayton insisted on thinking hard about choosing board members. He warned against a board of 'good old boys' or 'old chums'. One of his successors as chairman, Roger Hale, put it strongly: 'Don't join a board because "we're all buddies!"' Dayton also believed in succession planning. According to Bill Dietel, when choosing a board member Dayton would always ask, 'Is this person a potential chair?' And if two members were being recruited, 'one of them had to be a potential chair'. This succession planning avoided squabbles over who was next and also prevented boards from ducking decisions about leadership by 'kicking the decision down the field'.

Dayton was a stickler about what he might have called 'good board manners' which applied to boards of any kind and organizations of any size. According to Stephen Salyer there was an explicit 'Dayton's Law of Good Board Behaviour'. It involved, for instance, not leaving a board meeting to attend to other business or to return a phone call. (Dayton would have come down hard on today's mobile phone and social media obsessives.) As he put it: 'You wouldn't do this if you were serving on a

"Fortune 500" board. This is no different. Focus on the meeting. Give it your full attention.'

Salyer recalls a revealing occasion when Dayton was attending an APR sub-committee meeting chaired by a board member, Jon Lovelace. As it began, Lovelace's PA came into the boardroom to say that a major Hollywood executive needed to talk to him 'urgently'. As he prepared to slip out of the meeting he was chairing to take the call, Jon glanced sideways to where Ken Dayton sat, face lowered, the veins in his temple twitching with anger. Lovelace looked up and told his PA: 'Tell Mr Eisner I will have to call him back.' A later APR chairman told me of an influential board member who indulged in muttered conversations with a colleague during board presentations. Finally, the chairman openly rebuked the disrupter: 'We have a lot to talk about, but not while others are talking.' It was necessary; it worked. Sometimes such directness is essential.

My own experience of Ken Dayton as chairman was of a person of great charm, strong principles, sure sense of purpose, personal modesty, real generosity and strength of mind. Dayton conducted board business with directness, clarity and apparent simplicity. He believed too that members needed to know one another personally as well as professionally. After all, they met relatively infrequently as a board. Good decisions might not be made by a room full of strangers to one another. Board social gatherings in Minneapolis, with wives and partners, often took place at Ken and Judy's modernist house, its white walls hung with contemporary paintings. Typically, they had chosen their architect after a personal world-wide search; they chose their own paintings too. I have never known two rich people use their wealth so well and flaunt it so little. Bonding among board members in such an environment was strong as a result because the Daytons' hospitality made it easy. It was an aspect of how to manage governance itself in human terms and I made several good friends as a result.

A touch of social manipulation should never be undervalued in harmonizing board social dynamics. Bill and Linda Dietel made a practice of directing trustees to sit next to difficult or disruptive board members. Dietel recalls with satisfaction: 'It worked more often than you might imagine.'

On one occasion, Daytonian principle and practice took my breath away. On 20 October 1997, at an APR board meeting at the Stanhope Hotel in New York, the opening session began with a mutual review of one another's performance by the chair and the chief executive. This process was a 'Dayton favourite', one he practised regularly, insisting the CEO should pull no punches in judging how well he, the chair, had performed in his role over the previous year. In this case, the mutual assessment was between the then chair, Bill Dietel, and the CEO, Steve Salyer. I sat breathless as each examined the other's performance in measured, well-mannered, collegiate but searching terms. There was no personal point-scoring, no hidden malice, no concealed agenda, equally no evasion either. It was at once admirable because of its rigour, uncomfortable because of the extreme nature of the scrutiny required.

I tried without success to imagine the Chairman and the Director-General of the BBC carrying out such an exercise in front of the BBC Board of Governors. My imagination gagged at seeing either the tissues of evasion and pretence emerge from both mouths or the blood on the carpet that honesty would have demanded. My heart regretted that such an exercise – almost Calvinist in the rigour of its self-examination – had not been undertaken. My mind judged that the BBC would have been better governed if it had.

It remains a fact that few boards have had the stomach to undertake such severe Daytonian self-criticism. It was principled to the point of austerity. Even Bill Dietel, a very close colleague of Dayton's, both on and off the APR/PRI board, thought that full public review was too hard for many, not suitable for some. (He recalls as chief executive and president of the highly influential Rockefeller Brothers Fund [RBF], he had no reviews of performance in 17 years working for the Rockefellers.) At American Public Radio, Dietel as chair used to review performance with Steve Salyer but privately and informally: 'How are things going? Tell me the good things, the bad things.'

For Salyer himself, deep-dyed in Daytonian governance, relationships between chair and CEO came down to five principles: there should be 'no surprises' between them; there had to be tolerance of disagreement; if things were going wrong, it was essential to talk 'while we can do something about it'; there should be no rule by 'diktat'; and boards needed openness to work well, they could not do so if wrapped in ambiguity.

A major question arises: if an organization's governance is good, will this alone assure success in its performance? In the 1990s, American Public Radio grew from 19 full-time employees and some $3 million in revenues to more than 40 full-time employees and $20 million in revenues. After adopting a new mission, it announced the internationalization of its programming and purpose by changing its name to Public Radio International (PRI). It amended its charter to become a 'publisher' of programming, not just a distributor. Funds were raised to initiate ground-breaking programmes such as *The World* (international news) in cooperation with BBC World Service, *Classical 24*, (a 24-hour rolling classical music stream) and the weekly radio programme, *This American Life*. Each development represented a major advance in a pioneering decade.

In retrospect, that looks like consistent progress in line with the original mission and purposes. I also recall hiccoughs, frustrations and delays and a board driven by purpose and professionalism. Was this progress achieved by the rigorous governance principles defined and implemented by Ken Dayton and his successors, Bill Dietel, Roger Hale and others?

Did good governance deliver business success? Is it a sufficient condition for doing so? Of and by itself, it is unprovable. I do not believe that the transformation of a tiny Midwestern radio network into a major player on the US national media scene would have happened without a serious, rigorous foundation in the way it was governed. Governance supported and supervised management, it was as simple as that. It needed thought, belief and work and was striking to witness in action. Throughout, I felt that I was witnessing a specifically American approach to board governance.

By the late 1980s, leaders of not-for-profits across the United States had begun to notice that something special was happening in Minnesota – striking new ideas about governance for their world. Ken Dayton was acquiring a wide reputation as a guru on the subject. In 1987, 'The Independent Sector', a coalition of 700 national non-profit organizations, published his seminal paper, 'Governance is Governance'. Over the years, it became one of their most popular publications. In just a dozen pages, Dayton set out the accumulated wisdom and experience of a lifetime in the governance of both business corporations and non-profits. He insisted governance was not to be confused with management and that 'governance in the not-for-profit sector is absolutely identical to governance in the for-profit sector'. It needed a businessman to put the point so strongly – both propositions were original and unfashionable.

First, Dayton warned of deficiencies in not-for-profit boards, where either the paid executive surrendered its powers to the chair, or where chairs and boards, volunteers one and all, gladly usurped executive responsibilities. 'Why,' he raged, 'do so many corporate directors grow horns when they become trustees? Why do they intrude on what should be management decisions?' His answer was that a vacuum of executive authority would always be filled by someone, and at a cost: 'Any institution – for-profit or not-for-profit – that has an all-powerful Chair or a weak CEO is an institution in trouble or surely is one headed for trouble.'

Dayton insisted on the separation of powers and authority between chair and CEO. If the roles were combined, as often they were, the result would be 'dictatorship'. The correct relationship would be one where 'the Chair becomes the CEO's partner in making a great board'. Always a person to practise what he preached, Ken added from his own experience: 'I came to the conclusion that the only role of a trustee of the Minnesota Orchestral Association was the care and feeding of the Music Director.' Few would dare to put it in such an apparently self-effacing way.

In his paper, Dayton expected the chair to define a 'position description' of the CEO, adding that the executive should also spell out what he or she expected of the board! 'Pretty gutsy,' commented Dayton, 'but I'm a firm believer in getting my principles and convictions out on the table right from the very start.' A stickler for hard thinking about the size, age, composition, diversity and committee structure of the board, Dayton insisted on rotation of board members and chairs after stated periods of service: 'There is no such thing as the indispensable person, particularly the indispensable volunteer.'

Dayton concluded where he began: 'Governance is governance and management is management and the difference between the two must be clearly understood and accepted.' And finally, his unifying call: 'Governance is governance no matter what the institution – be it government, corporation or arts institution.' It reminded NfP boards that their conduct had to be on a level with those of major corporations, while corporations were reminded that their governance was not of itself better than that of the NfPs. Making money or not making money was not the issue or a defining characteristic. Only someone who had worked and served at the highest levels in both business and the arts could state such an unfashionable truth with such clarity and authority.

Dayton had a special warning for executives in the non-profit sector, those who said they didn't want a board 'looking over my shoulder, second-guessing me, reviewing my performance'. To any such executive, he advised, 'If you really want to build that institution into a dynamic force in society, they can do it so much more effectively if you have a dynamic, effective board.' Supervision, review and challenge were essential elements in the path to good performance.

Ken Dayton's observations have a pleasing directness and a deceptive simplicity. His advice has no theory in it, no abstractions, just an attractive clarity of thought which should compel acceptance. Yet, over the years, the evidence is that even with the best of advice available to them, many American NfP boards still struggle to put it into practice.

'Board Source' is the leading American organization focussed on 'strengthening and supporting NfP boards'. Founded in 1988, its influential 2017 survey of 1,300 NfP boards – 'Leading with Intent' – showed significant gaps between best practice in theory and in reality. Where boards were judged to be a 'collaborative team', more than half found social time for their members. But where boards judged themselves as not working in a collaborative way, only a fifth included opportunities for social get togethers. Was this cause or effect?

The survey found that boards had made no progress in improving the diversity of their membership in previous years. With 90 per cent of board chairs and 84 per cent of board members described as 'Caucasian', it is hardly surprising that 75 per cent of executives found the situation unsatisfactory. More executives than chairs believed that better diversity improved board performance, but only a quarter of them put 'improved diversity on the board' as a 'top three' priority. There were few signs of significant improvement in the offing. These numbers represent a serious gap of values between chairs and executives.

Since boards, chairs and CEOs were in a sense reporting on themselves in the 'Board Source' survey, the great majority judged their internal culture as good, believed that board members listened to one another and that members put the organization's interests uppermost and praised their own collective 'clear vision, enthusiasm and commitment'.

Later in the survey, cracks in this apparent complacency began to show. During meetings, rather than concentrating on mission, strategy and performance, 40 per cent of boards complained of the time spent on 'routine reporting'. While almost all had a strategic plan, barely 50 per cent thought they reviewed actual performance against the strategy. The most concerning part of the survey covered assessment of the chair's performance. Only 60 per cent of board members thought their chair had a constructive relationship with the CEO. Just 50 per cent thought the chair created an environment which built trust. And an alarming 40 per cent doubted the chair resolved conflicts and built compromise. These should be deeply worrying findings.

What the 2017 'Board Source' survey seemed to reveal is that most NfP boards in the United States knew how they ought to act and behave in theory. They had read the manuals, knew the official prescriptions, but a disturbingly large number still fell down on several functions that were regarded as essential, indeed routine to good governance practice.

Ken Dayton had written his report in 1989, no doubt reflecting the life and times of the era. The 'Board Source' survey of 2017 reported on the snapshot it took of how many NfP boards felt and behaved in 2015. Was there a way of exploring the quarter-century gap between Dayton's principles and current practices? How much of a gap was there? After all, my own direct experience of American-style governance was comparatively distant, narrow and perhaps unduly influenced by the atypically practical and severe approach of the APR board. I decided to update my own impressions by consulting four of the good colleagues I had worked with on the APR/PRI boards and to pool their wide experience. This would surely get me closer to current American practices of board governance.

Bill Dietel, founder of philanthropic advisory service Dietel & Partners, succeeded Dayton as chair of APR. Dietel's successor, Roger Hale – one-time president of Tenant Corporation – has been involved in human rights, disarmament and environmental organizations. Lawrence Wilkinson advised NfPs on governance and continued to be a board member of Public Radio International. Stephen Salyer followed up his 17 years as CEO of APR/PRI with 13 years as president of the Salzburg Global Seminar in Austria. Collectively, they had witnessed scores of organizations in the United States wrestle with problems and practices of governance. So, how did the scene look today through their eyes?

For a start, how would they define the characteristics of the 'Good Chair'? In Dietel's experience, the chair was always thinking about the major concerns facing the organization. Ideally, they would be very 'self-conscious' (or self-aware) of what the organization needed. He recalls that Ken Dayton would apparently start his morning shave by asking himself, 'What am I going to do today to be helpful to APR, to Minneapolis, or to the Walker Art Gallery?' He added a further warning from Dayton about where the board's focus should lie. The mission should come first and a board should not allow 'accumulation of capital to dominate board activities', a significant warning from a businessman. In other words, money was not the first and overriding concern. He went on to warn of the tension between the financial needs of an organization and the role that good governance could play in solving them. Proper governance was a necessary condition of a successful organization but it could never be a sufficient condition by itself.

Lawrence Wilkinson saw the 'Good Chair' as leader and collaborator who coached the CEO but learned as well. Roger Hale emphasized the need to keep balance on the board by restraining naturally dominant members and encouraging the more reserved, who were sometimes intimidated by the overly formal atmosphere of meetings. Hale recalled a member of an arms control board he chaired, where the member contributed very little over several years. After taking him aside and urging him to speak up, the once-silent member became a valuable contributor.

Hale also cautioned against enthusiastic board members who so mastered details of the organization's activity that their interventions went beyond supervision and ended up interfering in operational detail. His horror was reserved for a board concerned with airport operations, where it was filled with former pilots who went into such 'excruciating detail' that they made life virtually impossible for the executives. These members confused supervision with operations, a fundamental error in governance, and had to be brought into line by an effective chair.

While chairing The Center for Victims of Torture, Hale had a board made up almost entirely of human rights lawyers. Dedicated, knowledgeable and authoritative as they were, they were hopeless as a board, with 'no idea' of governance or board responsibilities such as fundraising. Their only expertise was in human rights and they were much less effective for their cause as a result.

What would a 'Bad Chair' look like? Worryingly, they are not hard to find. Lawrence Wilkinson suggested that the shared characteristics of bad chairs include holding strong views about the organization, imposing them, not responding to ideas and refusing to alter their approach through learning and experience. A truly bad chair, he concluded, got involved in operations, placed favourites on the board, created factions and ended up being destructive. Faced with such a chair, he had just one piece of advice: 'Beat a retreat.'

The dilemma faced by an executive when confronted by an overweening chair was different and more acute. Bill Dietel had two such experiences. As principal of the Emma Willard School for Girls in Troy, New York, the oldest school preparing females for higher education in the English-speaking world, he found his chair was constantly eroding his direct responsibilities and functions. It was necessary to stand up. 'Either I go or he goes,' he told the board. They backed him.

More dramatically still, Dietel had to face up to no less a figure than Nelson Rockefeller, who returned to the Rockefeller Brothers Fund (RBF) after a spell as Vice-President of the United States. Itching for something to do, Rockefeller tried to re-draw the functions and responsibilities of the chair in the expectation that he would be voted in as chair. This would have usurped authority from Dietel as director of RBF, effectively demoting him unilaterally to chief operations officer. Dietel warned the board he would quit if this diminution of his position and responsibilities was approved. Within 90 minutes, they endorsed his position and authority. I can think of few better examples of an executive necessarily standing up to an over-powerful chair.

My former colleagues had less to say about the way CEOs should treat their boards. One cautioned that they should not drone out presentations where the information was already provided in board papers, a besetting sin of executives the world over. Another urged executives not to 'swamp boards' with numbers – the right, useful numbers were needed to assess strategy, not all the numbers which risked straying into details of management. When one particular finance director was urged to reduce the complexity of their presentations they became more effective. A well-run board was defined as one 'where the staff speak very little and the board speak a lot'. It's a simple and reliable indicator.

Perhaps insecure CEOs might use deliberate information overload as a tactic to divert board attention from strategic matters. Perhaps it demonstrated a kind of passive-aggressive attempt to remind the board who really ran the show. Either way, it suggested executive weakness and insecurity rather than confidence. A good chair had an important role in managing such behaviours.

The foundation of the triangle of good governance is the board itself. Why join one at all, my friends mused. If you did, they urged, take it seriously, do the homework, give it the time and remember that you exercise 'fiduciary responsibilities' – you are not there to talk about the nuts and bolts of everyday business. Care about the organization's mission, know what it is for a start. Make your skillsets freely available and know where they can be most useful.

In sessions organized by the Salzburg Global Seminar, which Stephen Salyer has directed for 13 years, they introduced the notion of the 'Courageous Director'. How should they behave? The conclusion was that they needed enough knowledge to exercise their accountability responsibilities. They should ask themselves 'What questions should I have asked?' at a meeting. Were they right to have been satisfied with the answers? Did they press sufficiently for good answers? Salzburg summed up the notion and practice of the 'Courageous Director' by asking: 'Are board members ready to be "uncomfortable" and to make management "uncomfortable" though never in a vicious or belittling way?'

This might be asking too much and could indeed be the wrong thing to expect of any board. Remember what sort of people the directors are. One colleague explained why boards were reluctant to engage in much self-scrutiny: 'People who sit on boards have usually achieved a lot in their lives. They are accomplished people. They are used to governing organizations. They do not need self-scrutiny!' The 'Courageous Director' remains a potent challenge to board behaviour in the future. It was expressed differently by the counsel for a major Washington institution: 'It is not enough to bring to board service a good heart, there must also be an informed mind.' To which I would add an informed mind placed at the service of the organization.

The President of the American Museum Trustee Association (MTA), Mary Baily Wieler, answered her own question, 'What is a strong board member?' by offering the '4 Ws': 'Willingness to work; wisdom about the field; wealth to support the museum; and "wallop", defined as the ability to mobilize quickly and effectively'. These, too, are calls to action.

The frequently unexplored issue on boards, especially American ones, is the part that the acquisition and possession of money should play. When Stephen Salyer told his first Salzburg Seminar board meeting in November 2005 that everyone would be expected to contribute to an annual fund, he was roundly informed that the idea was 'too American'. He insisted and succeeded. A British friend working in the United States recalls with wonder how boards in the United Kingdom were 'indignant' at being asked for financial support. For my part, I knew that as a full member of the PRI Board I could not let the 'annual fund appeal' simply pass by as if I were somehow exempt because it was not part of my (mainly) British board culture. Indeed, it was part of US board expectation, which I accepted to the best of my ability.

Marti Segal, the all-wise New York arts advocate and Chairman of Lincoln Center, may have offered the pithy observation that in the United States board membership amounted to 'Give, Get, or Get off'. That's to say: give money yourself, find others who will give or else leave the board, an approach that the seventeenth-century philosopher Thomas Hobbes might have dismissed as 'nasty, brutish and poor'. From my own experience, and observation of US boards, I adapted the definition slightly to 'Get on (the board), Give (money), Get (others to give), Get Off (the board)'. Yet I have always seen this as a reductive and transactional way of describing what should be behaviour that engages generosity of spirit and not only in terms of cash. And Dayton warned that in the interests of 'diversity', boards needed members with multiple skills who could neither 'give' nor 'get'. This did not mean they had nothing to offer, board membership was not only for the rich.

The money question does not go away so easily; it is not only about giving and getting. Money, said one board member, was 'not a qualification for board membership.' This seemed to pre-figure another not unknown attitude on 'Not-for-Profit' boards, according to another: 'a certain disdain for people with money'. It overlooked the fact that members with money had contacts to offer beyond their own direct philanthropy; they might know others with funds, whether personal, philanthropic or corporate, and probably had further access to contacts who could 'open doors' to money. They could also have considerable skills unconnected to giving or getting money. Yet unease about money lurks on many American NfP boards. Some people were known to join a board as a way of making business contacts. Naturally, your own range of contacts would be significantly increased in doing so but that should be an incidental benefit rather than a prime reason for joining. Others had 'got rich quickly' and were 'endowed with a sense that they were really wise and smart'. Such individuals often displayed 'immodest opinions' and indulged in 'preaching, not learning'. In other words, they threw their weight around. Such characteristics might be displayed most acutely by young members who had made money. Every board seeks younger members (the majority age on American NfPs is between 50 and 64), yet the affluent young were often seen as slow to master the complexities and conventions of board conduct and responsibilities. 'Don't be impatient with them,' advised one former colleague. 'The young will be valuable on your board. Put them with a mentor to help them learn and adapt.'

In a few cases, success in business produced a perverse result: venture capitalists have been known to become ultra-conservative once they get on a board. 'They took risks in their own businesses,' observed one colleague, 'but became very conservative about risk on a NfP.' Was this just a more acute version of the frustration expressed by Derek Bok, President of Harvard: 'When businessmen walk into a non-profit boardroom, they leave 3/4 of their brains at the door.'

There was a further perspective for me to explore in the world of American boards: that of the great arts and culture institutions. Two at least have been run by Britons who could set their US experience in the context of the British arts world: Malcolm Rogers at the Museum of Fine Arts, Boston (MFA) and Sir Clive Gillinson at Carnegie Hall, New York.

Rogers arrived as director of MFA in 1993 after failing to secure the directorship of the National Portrait Gallery (NPG) in London. Once there, he turned a short-lived disappointment into a highly successful 21-year reign, bringing to it the full range of skills, artistic and managerial, now considered essential in modern cultural leadership. Faced with the task of raising some $70 million each year to keep the museum working, he enjoyed the advantages of a 'high net worth' US board. All gave money and many of them donated works of art or funds for art purchase. This led to a great feeling of 'ownership' within the museum family, of being 'stakeholders' or perhaps even 'shareholders' in the MFA. Rogers found the sense of civic responsibility backed by active philanthropy to be very high among the nearly 80 board members (few would welcome handling a board of such a size, no matter how wealthy).

On this strong foundation, Rogers and the MFA board raised the requisite millions each year, acquired funds for and built a new wing, grew attendances and memberships, expanded programming and created a sense of contact with the community by making it a museum for all, with 1,500 volunteers and the longest opening hours of any major US museum. 'Excellence for all' was Rogers' watchword, not elitism. The underlying paradox, a particularly American one, was that the 'excellence for all' was provided by the moneyed 'elite' few.

What Rogers could not have bargained for on his arrival was that he had to develop new skills as diplomat and politician in order to manage the board. Reconciliation of conflicting opinions and priorities came centre stage in his life. Certainly, board members gave generously but they did not all give for the same purposes. In the matter of museum policies individuals often supported their own priorities and interests rather than the civic and artistic mission of the organization, as defined in a succession of strategic plans, all of which had been voted unanimously by the board. The unacknowledged gap between seeing themselves as 'stakeholders' – those with a responsibility to the institution and its strategic direction as expressed in the strategic plans – and those who felt they were 'shareholders' – implying a right to determine its direction and purposes according to their personal agendas – was a problematic one. Such divisions required careful and subtle management on the part of the director, and strong leadership on the part of the chairman and president of trustees (which varied from individual to individual). Suddenly, 'stakeholders', 'shareholders' and 'ownership' became terms fraught with complexity, ambiguity and confusion.

The life of any director, especially in the United States, can be made more complicated by the very fact that many of his or her board move in the same social circles. Creating a diverse board of independent thinkers and movers and uniting them behind a shared vision along the lines of good governance practice is almost impossible. Even a strong chair might find it hard to 'move on' an ineffective trustee with whom they were in business or with whom they played golf or skied. 'The rich are different,' it has always been said, 'they have money'. To which I would add: 'They all know one another'. Governance and management are frequently entangled and the need for separation was poorly understood by some. MFA Boston was a huge success but its performance may have been suboptimal because of the lack of clarity and leadership in the matter of the divided responsibilities of director and board.

If Rogers proved a wily tactician, he also knew how to play the public role of director as had Roy Strong at the National Portrait Gallery. It was a performance. He was 'on stage' before his audience, whether his board or the wider community. What must they see as they observed him? He was, Rogers said, 'always positive, always smiling, always hard-working, invariably positive: "Yes, I'll get that done!"' It was also a study in a further part of governance: know the board and board leadership, and keep them close.

At Carnegie Hall in New York, Clive Gillinson arrived as executive and artistic director in 2005 after 21 years as the successful MD of the London Symphony Orchestra. His experience of another powerful, rich and engaged US board emerges as subtly different from that of Malcolm Rogers. With significant Latino, Black and Asian representation, Gillinson claims it is the 'most diverse' in the City. He has worked effectively with two chairs and when he and another chair fell out in a very public way, the Carnegie board backed Gillinson. He had by then established his credentials as a person who habitually explained, persuaded and responded to searching examination from his board, an approach learned at the outset of his tenure.

At his very first board meeting, Gillinson presented Carnegie Hall trustees with plans for two ambitious projects: one, an annual, city-wide festival of music, dance, literature, film and theatre, partnering with other leading New York cultural institutions. The second was a two-year fellowship programme to be created with the Juilliard School for the finest postgraduate musicians who wanted a portfolio career of high performance combined with outreach and access based on their musical excellence. It was a daring start to his tenure.

The Carnegie Hall board liked the ideas but thought them too ambitious to carry out at the same time. Gillinson then asked permission to meet two of the doubters in person to try and persuade them that both projects were doable. After a coffee meeting, the first trustee explained: 'I now believe in both of your projects and your strategy for implementing them and raising funding for them. I would hate you to have come so far for nothing, so here is a cheque for $500K.' It had been a 10-minute walk from Gillinson's office in the Hall.

The second trustee invited Gillinson to lunch, challenged every aspect of the strategy and its funding. Once satisfied, she pledged support of $1 million. Both projects proceeded and proved successful. Both were utterly American experiences.

Gillinson's decade-plus years in New York give him perspective on board life in London. He accepts that British boards will never necessarily be as personally wealthy as American ones. Even among the 'high-net-worth' individuals in both countries, there are different models, traditions and expectations of giving. His experience is that US boards behave with great rigour, especially in the 'fiduciary' committees such as audit, finance and operations, governance and security. British boards will, he believes, need to define their responsibilities more thoroughly and this will include defining expectations of giving. For chief executives the lesson is the need to meet critical scrutiny and to answer it. The role of trustees will be to provide it.

Lurking behind the eternal money question I detected a deeper issue stirring, a feeling of 'entitlement' – that the act of giving money, however apparently disinterested, brought with it an expectation of privileges for the donor. Privileges of opinion, of influence, even of an actual say in the cultural direction of the organization. Arts institutions need the money but Bill Arning, outgoing director of the Contemporary Arts Museum Houston (CAMH), has written about the human and professional costs that meeting these expectations of entitlement can inflict.

Trustees need looking after, for sure. Some expect to be looked after; museum staff have to take up this extra responsibility, in effect a further burden. 'Taking donors to the Venice Biennale or Documenta will often be very enjoyable,' wrote Arning. 'Nothing cements a donor relationship better than an exquisite meal on Giudecca.' This effort involves a cost. After several years of active donor 'cultivation', Arning warned, 'the exhaustion can be extreme.' The price of less diligent 'cultivation' might well be lower funding.

For some, the problem of an unacknowledged sense of 'donor entitlement' among certain board members needed thoughtful management. If special treatment was expected, how should it be met? How should executives respond to such demands given that many arts institutions have come to rely on this 'unrestricted' funding? What one executive named 'making nice' to entitled people was now part of the scene and acceptable if it involved free tickets, reception invitations and 'behind the scenes' access. But lines needed to be drawn, with parameters defined showing no amount of giving entitled the donor to more than a single vote. And any trespassing on artistic matters to suit a donor's whims would have to be firmly resisted.

Blessed with generous trustees and supporters at Carnegie Hall, Clive Gillinson was well aware of the fine line between a sense of 'ownership', which you wanted to encourage, and an assumption of 'possession', which you had to resist. His watchword was 'Know what you believe in, get people to back what you believe in.' He listened to potential funders' interests, aligned them with the Hall's mission and objectives and tried to harmonize them. But he insisted that ultimately, there could be no compromise: 'Money follows vision. Never do things you do not believe in just to get donations. If the donor really won't fund your organization's mission, it is important to have the courage to stay with the mission and forgo the donation if you cannot persuade them to back what you believe in.' The lesson must be that donor generosity should not carry entitlement with it. A good giver is a good giver, a disinterested one does not regard giving as part of a transaction where they get something in return.

I found that the lessons of my American board experience sank in for many years after the mere decade that I was involved in it directly. It was additional to what I had learned from the National Portrait Gallery. Many elements were similar; the differences were subtler but real. I was struck by the almost innocent observation from Roger Hale: 'For five years after I retired in 1999, I participated in "governance" and "directorship" panels. I always made a point of interpersonal dynamics in boardrooms. I've read countless articles and books about governance and board behaviour and only once did I encounter any statement about that. I am convinced that is the most important aspect affecting board behaviour.'

In other words, after all the rules, the requirements, the manuals, the guidance, the rubrics, the inductions, the practice of good governance simply turns on how people behave towards one another in the boardroom. There is no legislation for that: good behaviour cannot be taught, it must be learned.

REFLECTIONS

The invitation to join the board of American Public Radio (APR) was unexpected not sought, but nonetheless became a valuable experience.

APR began as a small competitor to its well-established National Public Radio (NPR). In defining its purpose and mission, APR thrived and became Public Radio International (PRI). PRI took governance seriously.

Two-thirds of trustees were independents, only one third were member affiliates.

Those who are direct beneficiaries of the activity or might have a pecuniary interest in it should not be a majority on the board.

No PRI trustee served for reasons of social vanity or business advantage, all were driven by commitment to PRI's success.

PRI's founding chair, Kenneth Dayton, insisted the trustees' role was to appoint, support and question their chief executive in the delivery of the mission. They were not to second-guess the executive.

The PRI board understood Dayton's mantra that 'Governance is governance and management is management'.

Boards should not be made up of 'good old boys' or 'old chums'. Trustees should be chosen with a view for one of them to be capable of becoming chair in due course.

Many 'not-for-profit' (NfP) board members judged that their chair did not have a good relationship with the CEO.

Many also believed their chair did not create an atmosphere of trust.

A 'Good Chair' keeps a balance on the board, reining in the assertive and bringing out the reticent.

Boards composed of experts in the field know little of governance and may end up obstructing the executives.

A 'Bad Chair' has favourites, meddles in operations and allows factions to grow.

Chief executives should not swamp boards with too many numbers. While the right kind of information can be very economical, providing too much information can be a passive-aggressive way of avoiding scrutiny.

A 'Courageous Director' asks questions of the executive, considers if they were the right questions and whether the answers were accepted too easily.

Boards need younger members. Offering mentoring in governance makes them more effective.

Good behaviour on a board demands giving full attention to the business in hand and not being diverted by phone calls or emails. Being a trustee is a serious appointment and requires attention and commitment.

Boards that give time to socializing together are more pleasant and tend to be more effective.

Boards should review their performance regularly. Chairs should review the CEO regularly. A brave and rigorous board may choose to have chair and CEO engage in mutual open assessment of their performance. This is not for every board and certainly not for the faint-hearted.

Chairs and CEOs should work on the basis of 'no surprises'. Difficulties should be discussed while there is time to put them right.

Good governance will assist successful performance and cannot by itself overcome a difficult business environment.

Good governance works on the same principles in the business and NfP sectors. It is not different because the financial environment is different.

Boards should not spend all their time looking at the finances. Governance is more than that: watch the mission.

An all-powerful chair or a weak CEO, let alone the two together, means an institution is heading for trouble.

The CEO should make clear the expectations they have of the board. Tricky to do, but better than lack of clarity about expectations.

Trustees who give should do so in line with the organization's mission and purposes rather than to satisfy their own wishes. 'Get on, Give, Get, Get off' is a reductive view of the complexity, riches and potential satisfactions of board membership.

Feeling a sense of 'ownership' of an arts institution does not mean that you can call the shots or influence decisions.

Being a 'stakeholder' in an institution involves accepting responsibility for its performance. Seeing yourself as 'shareholder' in an arts institution does not mean you know how to run it, that you have a right to say how it should be run or that you should try to run it.

A wise CEO tells the board what they are doing, when, how and why they are doing it and persuades them that they deserve support.

Money should not buy privilege on a board. A good giver does not expect anything back from the institution – in favours, privileges or power. Also, a good giver feels no sense of 'entitlement' to special treatment. It may be offered but should not be expected.

A sense of entitlement is a kind of vanity.

American boards expect to give and do so. A diverse, balanced board still leaves room in its composition for those who cannot give.

NfP boards should value those with money not only for themselves but for the contacts they may make and bring.

Looking after donors – 'making nice' to them – is good practice but takes its toll on staff.

Most bad board behaviour is about how people react to and with one another. You cannot codify good behaviour in any governance rule book.

A good board member demonstrates the 'Four Ws' – Willingness to work; Wisdom about the field; Wealth to support the mission; 'Wallop' – the ability to mobilize quickly and effectively when needed.

3

English National Opera: Board Without Power (1994–2004)

Interviews with

Sir Richard Aikens, board member, High Court judge

Charles Alexander, board member, merchant banker

Sir John Baker, Chairman, English National Opera (ENO); Chairman,
National Power (1987–97)

Bob Boas, board member, merchant banker

Sir Rodric Braithwaite, board member, diplomat

Lord (Tom) Chandos, board member

Sir Anthony Cleaver, board member; Chairman, IBM UK

Sally Groves, music publisher; wife of the late Dennis Marks, former BBC
Head of Music and General Director of English National Opera (ENO)

Theresa Lloyd, development consultant

Russell Willis Taylor, Managing Director, English National Opera (ENO)

Early in 1994, I was phoned by Dennis Marks, the recently appointed
General Director of English National Opera (ENO) at the Coliseum in

St Martin's Lane, London. Would I care to have lunch with him and the chairman, Lord Harewood, to discuss joining the Board of Trustees? This was an attractive thought. I knew Dennis well from years of contact and cooperation at the BBC and in London's musical scene. In 1986, we had worked together on a television programme covering the memorable return to his native Russia of the legendary virtuoso pianist, Vladimir Horowitz. I knew of Lord Harewood, former director of both the Royal Opera and ENO and editor of *Kobbe*, the authoritative reference book on opera. He knew, it seemed, every opera, every singer and conductor. What he had forgotten about the world of opera was more than most of us ever know. It seemed a rather special invitation.

We met for lunch in the Chairman's Retiring Room at the Coliseum on 27 January 1994. With sounds from the general dress rehearsal of Strauss' *Der Rosenkavalier* drifting in from the auditorium, the atmosphere was beguiling. I have always loved opera and had seen a great deal during my time as a National Serviceman serving in the army in West Germany in 1955–56. The conversation over lunch was about opera in general with, I suppose, thoughts about what I might bring to the board. I would have offered my personal love of opera and my practical record of almost a decade running the BBC World Service. Not that the lunch was any sort of interview even of the most informal kind, that was not how boards were formed in those days. The formalities and processes of governance were a few years away.

Of course I accepted the invitation to join. Writing two days later, Lord Harewood said how delighted the board was that 'you have agreed to join us'. He added: 'I don't think you will find the duties too onerous. We can probably absorb as much time as you care to give us but even that should not stretch you too far.' Seldom can a letter of invitation have proved so totally, though unintentionally, misleading. It ushered in a decade of on-stage brilliance, off-stage drama, financial crisis, political wrangling, public controversy involving the departure of three general directors and one chairman as the board struggled to reconcile the ambitions of artistic directors with the financial rigours of public funding. In the process, the conventions and rules of governance were tested and stretched to the limit. The capacity of even a serious and competent board to control – still less to shape – events was exposed. All of this would emerge in the years ahead.

At that stage, the background surrounding the ENO board was only bright. The company was basking in the afterglow of the so-called 'Power House' years when what was regarded as the 'dynamic triumvirate' of director Peter Jonas, producer David Pountney and conductor Mark Elder had dominated the scene with productions of dazzling and bewildering novelty, imagination and ingenuity. Two years previously, the British government had bought the lease of the Coliseum and presented it to ENO as its London home, a performance palace as a gift for sure. The Harewood/Marks team looked professional, serious and creative and likely to build on this inheritance. But the foundations for a successful future were, it would soon turn out, weak.

They began at the very top with George Harewood, a supremely knowledgeable and well-connected character. 'Splendid in almost every way,' recalled one board member, 'a valuable figure head.' Then the reservations crept in. 'An old-fashioned man,' observed another, with 'views that were beginning to look old-fashioned'. The arts, he believed, had a 'right to exist' because they were a 'force for good'. Harewood had 'a sense of entitlement for the arts' – he considered finances to be no more important than they would be to 'the landowner of a big estate' (which he was). More worryingly, the chairman was thought to regard 'budget projections as a spending calculation', meaning the budget merely fired a starting pistol for expenditure, which of course was destined for the art. Admirable, attractive even as this approach sounded, ENO was on the verge of an era where such simplicities would no longer be adequate.

Charismatic, aristocratic figurehead as he was, this did not make Harewood a chairman in the governance terms that were beginning to emerge in the early 1990s. 'He had strong views on what made the company tick,' said a contemporary, 'but he had no experience of what was the orderly management of business. He clearly did not understand what a chairman's role was and what he did understand he found it difficult to come to terms with.' Tony Cleaver observed: 'I respected him but he was a very poor chairman.' He wondered if Harewood really wanted a board at all. Another added: 'He didn't keep order that I could see.'

Not to cast aspersions on the great man that he undoubtedly was, George Harewood then infringed upon two further cardinal principles of governance. First, he should not have moved from being chief executive of the company to becoming its chairman; all governance principles warn against this. Innovation cannot thrive within what could be mere protection of the status quo in the name of continuity. What Harewood knew was vast but it was not the right kind of knowledge for a non-executive chairman. He was a man of his time and that time had passed.

The second infringed principle was his relationship with the General Director, Peter Jonas. They were too similar, two men of the world of opera, steeped in the same outlook about the unchallengeable primacy of the arts. In the view of a businessman, Tony Cleaver, 'They were on the same page, too close.' The chairman/chief executive relationship was best governed on this view by the twin poles of 'partnership and separation', which is to say: 'We are totally on the same side until the day that I have to sack him.' Partnership and separation, a form of balance, but in a state of tension, the essential paradox of the highest level of successful governance.

If Harewood and Jonas had been too close, so too were Harewood and Dennis Marks. This benefited neither, but the incoming Marks was to be the loser. For a start, he inherited a legacy that was far from glittering, almost a poisoned chalice. The 'Power House' regime trailed crowds of critical glory but left a little-noticed £3 million deficit behind. Its most radical and once-praised productions proved unrevivable or otherwise lost money when they were relaunched. As the former diplomat, Rodric Braithwaite, a knowledgeable observer of opera, concluded: 'the [Power House] deserved their reputation. But by the end of their time they had exhausted their ideas. It is no criticism to say they were worn out. That happens.' He added: 'The "Power House" was a conjuring trick based on a very rickety foundation.'

In the decade that followed, saddled with the inherited debt, ENO never got into a stable period of balanced budgets but lurched from crisis to crisis. Succeeding managements bore the weight of these crises but their inheritance was compromised from the start. Marks' wife, the music publisher Sally Groves, insists that he was warned about the dire state of affairs he would inherit well before he took over: 'ENO finance staff were coming to Dennis in desperation, saying that lies were being peddled about the financial situation.'

Two questions arise: why did the board appoint Dennis Marks? And why did he accept the job despite being forewarned about the difficulties of the situation that he would face in a role of a size and type he had not previously carried out?

The second is more easily answered. Marks firmly believed in ENO and its mission of being a national company singing in English: two attractive principles – the idea of a company existing for the nation, singing in the national language. As a senior BBC executive, he had regularly telecast one ENO production every year. He knew that filling the 2,300 seats in the Coliseum night after night was not practicable; also that the house was the wrong size for Mozart, the facilities at the Coliseum were antiquated and wholly unsuited for the needs of repertory opera. But, says Sally Groves, 'he was undaunted, he was so thrilled by the idea of ENO.' If he went in with his heart open, his eyes and mind must have had to stay averted.

But why did the ENO board appoint him? Marks was musically knowledgeable, articulate, intellectual, enthusiastic. His track record at the BBC was of the highest class and he was known as a 'wheeler-dealer on projects and budgets which he believed in'. He looked and sounded practical. The board must have shelved their doubts about his lack of large-scale management experience. 'Wheeler-dealing in BBC corridors' was one thing, managing an enterprise of 500 people and a large building as well was quite another. They may also have disastrously misread the person Dennis Marks was. One board member described him as an 'arch-bureaucrat who was anti-bureaucracy', a confused judgement that got only the second part correct. Another concluded that after Peter Jonas 'we have had enough of the visionary', a further profound misunderstanding of their man. Yet they chose him.

Boards almost always recognize that the preferred candidate for an executive position lacks one or two main skills. They face three choices: to set aside their doubts, to decide the candidate will learn on the job, or to hope that existing colleagues will fill in the skills gaps. There is a fourth choice, seldom used: to recommend that the otherwise 'best' candidate should have specific training to remedy their deficiencies before they take over. In Sally Groves' view, Dennis Marks should have had training in 'team management, big management, eighteen months before he took over. By the time he got [to ENO], it was too late.'

Should the chairman have advised Marks to have management training? Harewood would hardly have been the person to think of it, let alone suggest it. It does not shift responsibility for subsequent difficulties away from Marks to say that the board's inability to recognize the scale of his management shortcomings and to find ways of remedying them was a failure of their governance responsibilities.

There was one further draught in the poisoned chalice of the 'Power House' years. According to his wife, Dennis Marks was taken aside by Peter Jonas and given one piece of advice: 'Never tell the board anything.' But Marks' later problems with the board cannot be laid solely or at all at Peter Jonas' feet. His own background from the BBC, where the non-executive Board of Governors was regarded by staff with universal and frosty disdain, will not have helped. There is no evidence that Marks took Jonas' comment seriously.

What of the board itself? I found a combination of two bankers, three businessmen, two civil servants, a judge and two philanthropists. With just two women and one ethnic minority in a board of fewer than two dozen, it was hardly diverse. It was definitely not stupid. More obviously, selection came through recommendation, invitation and friendship. I was a friend of Dennis Marks; three others were friends of an existing member. Tony Cleaver was invited to join by George Harewood 'over tea at the Athenaeum'. Criteria, process, selection, skillsets were wholly absent. This did not make it a bad board – it was one of the most serious and able that I ever sat on. But it was a board at a time of transition, said Rodric Braithwaite, 'from the old gentlemanly way of being on boards. It was not about being decorative, it was not enough to be nice or titled. It was not an end point in a career. We were becoming more orderly.' Soon, we would be put to the test.

Harewood's successor as chairman, John Baker, could not have been more different. Baker came from the most senior levels of the world of industry and business and was an open communicator with an active record of involvement in and interest in the arts. With wide experience of managing a board, he was very clear about how a chairman should act and behave. He insists he had 'no vision of putting a personal stamp on the organization.' If there was a public role to play, it was as a 'behind the scenes public face' linking the organization with staff and supporters. It was not to say in any sense, 'I am the company'. A later director, Russell Willis Taylor, interim then executive director from 1997–2000, judged him to care about the organization 'completely and tirelessly', adding 'he parked his ego at the door before a board meeting'.

Baker's expectations of his chief executive were equally distinct: he wanted clear managerial discipline established and a realistic judgement of the financial and political environment in which the company existed. Finally, he expected the entire chair/chief executive relationship to be governed by one overriding principle: 'Transparency in all things.' Reasonable as this may have sounded, ultimately, it proved too much to expect.

When John Baker was approached to join the board by two existing members, they told him there was a great deal that needed sorting out at ENO, no one else had the time to give to it, so would he 'have the time to give a hand?' As he put it: 'On that slippery basis I said "yes"'. Soon, he found himself chairman. Surveying the people around him, he detected a certain pattern in the types of board members: 'There were the cheerleaders who backed the artistic direction but were not interested in the money; others were concerned with ENO's sustainable future and were therefore very concerned with the money; and there were one or two nerds like me who were very interested in how the place was managed.' Not entirely by accident, however, the ENO Board did have strong representation of desirable skills, musical experts, business people and fundraisers. Baker added: 'But people got there by word of mouth rather than by deliberation.' Including himself.

One further way of parsing the board ran as follows: 'There are the suits, there are the luvvies. And there is Tusa – with the heart of a luvvie but the mind of a suit.' At all events, it was an easy board to lampoon. When Treasury Minister David Mellor, who signed over the Coliseum leasehold to ENO, joined the board in 1993, the *London Evening Standard* ran an unflattering double-page spread summing up the board as an establishment racket, its members, it alleged, driven only by vanity, too much spare time and the lure of free tickets. For ourselves in 1994, what was certainly a 'transitional board' in governance terms found the demands on our time, skills, energy and patience over the next decade to be increasingly demanding. No one could say we ever lacked motivation or commitment. Free tickets could never have compensated for the time, trouble and stress that were to be involved. I had no compunction about making use of them, though in any case John Baker later stopped the practice.

The scale and complexity of the problems ahead emerged at a Board Awayday weekend at Harewood House on 18 and 19 March 1994. Situated on the outskirts of Leeds, the house is an elegant eighteenth-century building filled with wonderful paintings and art, starting with the monumental Epstein marble piece of Jacob wrestling with the Angel. But at that time, the glories of art history could not distract from the realities of the present. Staring the board in the face was the condition of the theatre building itself. Wonderful as the British government's gift of the lease had been, it was known that the condition of the theatre left everything to be desired. It was summed up not long after by Richard Morrison in *The Times*: 'Its foyers and bars are tiny; its space for catering and corporate entertaining laughable; its rehearsal rooms non-existent; its air-conditioning Victorian; its plumbing Plantagenet.' In fact, the 'gift' of the Coliseum came with a huge bill attached – no less than £7 million in dilapidations liability. But government and opera company felt they had to act with some urgency. With the death from a heart attack of the owner of the Stoll Moss Theatre Group, Robert Holmes à Court, on 2

September 1990, there was a possibility that the Coliseum might be sold as a home for musicals, its original purpose. But that would have left ENO literally homeless.

With all the benefits of hindsight, it is remarkable that the board did not ask for a budget for restoration as part of the government's 'gift' package. They had a new home but couldn't afford to do it up. Bob Boas insists that it would have been completely unrealistic to expect additional money for renovation – the government had been strikingly generous already. Nevertheless, in the following years the 'gift' looked less like a dowry and felt more like an albatross weighing the company down. Worse still, with its clankingly awful plumbing, was it to be more like a Trojan Horse?

At Harewood, the board had a presentation from the development consultant Theresa Lloyd about the strength of funders' support for a major restoration of the Coliseum. It would have amounted to renovation rather than transformation, an indication of the essential repairs that needed doing. At an estimated cost of £60 million it looked poor value for money. The former TV executive and later Tory government minister Shaun Woodward proposed that, rather than tinker with an inefficient building, the board should explore the option of an entirely new opera house – a 'new build'.

This was high ambition but not unreasonable given that a mere refit would never make the Coliseum capable of meeting the demands of modern repertory opera. At first, the project had a following wind. The Arts Council of England (ACE), funders of first and last resort, contributed a sizeable £1.5 million for a major feasibility study by the consultants KPMG, with Terry Farrell as the architect. They concluded a brand-new site on the Thames South Bank immediately adjacent to Tower Bridge called Potter's Field was the preferred option. Lloyd consulted potential private and corporate donors and found them strongly encouraging: 'What mattered was what happened on stage and in the pit but since the Coliseum was not ideal and the support services were scattered all over London then it was a good idea to bring them all together on one site.' She concluded: 'They were unequivocally for a "new build". It would be the only brand-new, lottery-funded, ground-up, breakthrough building.' Bob Boas hoped the new 'house' would be adopted as a 'millennium project', but by the time the British government 'had blown £700 million on the Dome it was too late. ENO's "new build" would have been done for a quarter of the cost.' The story of ENO's project was to be wrecked by political interference and decision-making.

Having taken the decision to explore a new house, the board and management kept it under constant review. There was never a fixed consensus about the scheme. Charles Alexander, a banker, thought it was a 'real opportunity for a new start. The artistic case for Potter's Field was compelling, the commercial/business case less so. Would it have stood the test of whether it was feasible to build a new theatre? The cost would have been far more than £80 million.' But once committed to such a scheme, any failure to fund the capital project and more seriously, to agree funding for the actual musical programming within it would, he thought, have destroyed the company. Alexander was not the only member to feel that any risk assessment would have had to come down on the side of caution.

It did not help that the general director was heavily committed to a new house. Dennis Marks had good reasons for doing so. 'You can put as much gold and frills front of house but backstage, people are still pulling scenery with ropes' was how he put it. And there was a moral and welfare aspect to it, according to Sally Groves: 'He disliked the fact that those doing the work, who were making art, were still living and working in squalid conditions – that was wrong.' For the board, these considerations, strong as they were, unarguable as they might be, could not sway a high-cost, risk-filled decision.

Besides, they were taken aback by the hostility of the reaction to leaving the Coliseum led by the opera press and including David Mellor, the minister responsible for originally transferring the lease. Audience research too found that ENO supporters were wedded to arriving at Charing Cross or Waterloo for their opera night out and wholly unfamiliar with the whereabouts of Potter's Field – still less how they might get there. One well-connected outsider predicted that it would take existing loyal audiences the better part of a decade to get used to attending a new venue in a then remote, unconnected and unfamiliar location. London was a very different and less-connected city than it is today. The 'downside' of the risk assessment was getting longer and longer. No one spoke up for the vast opportunities that beckoned. (Today, the site is the venue for the fabulously successful Bridge Theatre.)

To this day, from the development perspective, Theresa Lloyd, admittedly not a board member, regards the ENO board's failure to back the project as a huge missed opportunity, showing a 'pusillanimous lack of guts by the Board.' In her experience, philanthropic investment followed vision and excellence, as Tate Modern demonstrated. World-class architects, she insists, would have fought over one another to design a new national opera house for the twenty-first century on a bend in the Thames in the greatest city in the world. But another observed sharply: 'The Board came to their senses.'

In any case, the politics of funding 'glossy new arts projects' were turning decisively against Potter's Field. Marks had hoped and believed that the incoming Blair 'New Labour' government would prove friendly to the arts. He failed – and he was not alone in this – to appreciate the extent of New Labour's antipathy to the arts and their modish, pseudo-egalitarian dedication to inclusive 'creativity' rather than what they rejected as 'elite' achievement. What could be more 'elitist' than building a new opera house? Early in the New Labour time in office, Tom Chandos was told by an adviser to the new Culture Secretary, Chris Smith, that their 'number one priority was to deliver a renewed Royal Opera House.' On this view, ENO was the casualty of a political decision rather than one about the substance of the project: 'ACE cut us off at the legs.' Bob Boas recalls that the Arts Council throughout was 'too political. They funded the feasibility report on the new build. When it was completed, they didn't even want to look at it. It was never discussed between ACE and ENO, we were just told it was out of the question. They behaved appallingly.' The case for a new house for ENO was, recalls another, 'blown away in the political gale'. It fell into the Secretary of State's 'pending tray' marked 'Too Difficult'.

In any tussle over funding ENO was always going to come off second best to the Royal Opera. Paradoxically, the worse the financial crisis at the ROH, a merry-go-round of resignations, a revolving door of coming and going chief executives, threats of bankruptcy, the worse the outlook for what were ENO's more modest ambitions. Besides, the ROH Board was better-connected, more politically influential, their financial supporters richer, funding prospects more secure. The anti-elitist world view of New Labour might just accommodate the need to save one failing opera house but not two. The fact that the 'non-elitist' opera house that was English National Opera was the one to be cast aside was an irony too far to be registered except with a wry shrug.

Given these complexities which played out during Dennis Marks' four-year tenure, was he over-committed to the new build? Tom Chandos believes that he was: 'He was very, very disappointed in not getting the building. It was the end of the affair.' Another judged he was 'devastated' by the decision.

The new build issue was a running sore for four years. It was not the only matter in hand. In the foreground, there was an existing opera company to run, operas to produce, a repertoire to refresh, imagination to fire, seats to fill, budgets to manage. This was Dennis Marks' job. Tom Chandos regarded him as 'mercurial but consistently right on the big things', adding, 'he was pretty visionary'. Most board members would, I think, endorse Rodric Braithwaite's considered judgement on the Marks regime: 'As far as artistic achievement was concerned, Dennis was a very good general director. *Soldaten* [by Bernd Alois Zimmermann] was one example of a courageous and successful production of a very rare work. Schnittke's *Life with an Idiot* was a failure but right for ENO to do it. Both were expensive but artistic institutions do have to take risks and these were justified. Productions were grand but never wasteful.' With a sense of perspective, Chandos observed, 'The best times were never as golden as they were painted but the worst times still had extraordinary quality!' Braithwaite's measured conclusion was that 'The artistic achievement under Dennis Marks was comparable with that of the "Power House".' Unfairly, such public and critical recognition never came Marks' way. Later, Nicholas Payne, his successor, generously paid tribute to the artistic legacy he inherited from Marks.

What went wrong? When John Baker joined the board in 1995 he knew that a great deal more than mere 'sorting out' was required at ENO. There was no time to take stock and plan decisions, he faced a complex set of pre-existing situations. Finance was a running sore with the company overlaid by the inherited deficit from the previous regime. Worse still, in the new chairman's view, the Arts Council, the prime funder, was from the outset never on the side of the company: 'It was clear that their policy was to keep us in hock. The moment we produced a surplus, the grant was reduced to keep us to a zero increase. So there was no room for manoeuvre.' Baker acknowledged Marks' determination in 'struggling with an impossible position'. Neither was helped by the politics surrounding the 'two opera houses' problem. From the start, existential questions about the company's very existence were being asked and there was nothing ENO could control or even influence very much in this all-too public debate.

It was perhaps inevitable in view of the public controversy that an inquiry should have been set up in 1994. Did we really need two opera houses side by side in London? Under Dennis Stevenson, it recommended a 'reduced role' for ENO, with 'reduced infra-structural support', weasel code words for a freelance rather than a permanent orchestra. Nothing came of it, but the strain placed on an already hard-pressed organization was huge. It was a 'major distraction' recalled one member.

Worse still, its treatment of Dennis Marks set the course of relations between ENO and the Arts Council on a steep downward trajectory. According to Sally Groves: 'Dennis would say, "There's this report coming over the horizon." I don't think he was even consulted. He never got any sight of what was in it. He only saw it on the eve of publication. It was a complete and utter stitch-up.' Making due allowance for the recollection of strong emotion, leaving Marks and ENO relatively remote from what were deeply damaging recommendations for the company's future had profound consequences.

Increasingly, tensions between the general director and the board turned on how to deal with this indifferent, even hostile, Arts Council. Charles Alexander saw it as a fundamental but honest disagreement about tactics over funding. What would be an acceptable outcome of these negotiations? 'Dennis wanted to fight for a three-year settlement, including an uplift for inflation. The Board thought that two years of a "stabilization" grant without an inflation increase was the best we would get. After two years, you "re-grouped" and started again.' That was how bureaucratic campaigns were fought, over time. As Alexander put it, 'the Board said "Let not the best be the enemy of the good." We became frustrated that Dennis could not accept the Board's interpretation of reality.' Others criticized what they saw as the Arts Council's refusal to take an objective decision about what ENO might need financially to fulfil its artistic vision. Instead, ACE negotiations over funding ENO were seen as all very ad hoc, on the lines of 'Can we give them a bit more, should we give them a bit less?' It was not felt to spring from a properly informed and thought-through decision.

Facing them was a general director with a settled and near-absolutist position. Partly, it was Dennis Marks being deeply political, recalls Charles Alexander: 'The need to stand up in defence of the publicly funded arts sector for the benefit of the greatest good for the greatest number.' Partly, it was sheer defiance, according to John Baker: 'Dennis had this mantra, "I don't mind if the company goes bankrupt because the politicians will always bail me out". In those words.' Partly, it was a high-risk bet that ENO could spend what it wanted and the ACE would give way. From Peter Jonas onwards, successive directors claimed that ENO was 'too big to fail'. Others in the arts world thought in a similar way.

Impossible as this was as a strategy, Baker, Cleaver and others pointed out to Marks that trading while knowingly insolvent was a criminal offence punishable by disqualification from holding a position as director of a public company. Several board members made it clear that any policy of deliberate bankruptcy to force ACE's hand would result in mass resignations.

If the tactical gap between chairman, board and chief executive was turning into a chasm, the temperamental gap of approach was even wider. Sally Groves recalls it like this: 'Dennis had no strategy for dealing with the Arts Council. He just fought head-on, fists up. If ACE didn't like it, Dennis said, "Tough!"' John Baker was very aware of how high feelings about the Arts Council ran: 'Dennis's policy was to hate them, to fight them, which was an absolutely lost cause.' Such attitudes led an embattled Marks to regard the board as 'appeasers' or in Charles Alexander's colourful imagery: 'He may have thought, "I was prepared to sit in Saint Martin's Lane and douse myself with petrol, why weren't they?"' To call the relationship 'very adversarial' would be a huge understatement. But who were the adversaries? The board or the Arts Council? Fighting on two fronts is always a bad idea. Then there was a third to make matters worse.

If such vastly divergent and mutually contradictory views about how to negotiate with the principal funder were an ill omen, Marks was finding the actual job, the task of running a 500-strong opera company, very demanding. He felt chained to his management desk, which kept him away from where he wanted to be: in the theatre, working with singers, conductors, producers, technicians in the engrossing tasks of mounting an opera production. He was thrown by the realization that while in his former world of television, a programme could always be deferred until it was ready, on the long-scheduled first night of an opera, 500 people all had to come together in a collective act of skill and will to get the show ready for curtain up. In the theatre, 2,300 people would be waiting for the curtain to go up. Board members had some understanding of the complexity of the operation. As the banker Bob Boas recognized, 'An opera company is one of the most difficult organizations to run. It is more difficult than most businesses.' No amount of sympathetic understanding could help Marks deal with the brutal everyday complexities. It was too late for that.

What the board did expect was complete openness about the state of the numbers. Even those without major commercial backgrounds expected nothing less than total frankness. How could trust at the top be built and kept without it? It is easy to underestimate and disregard the fragility of the forecasts on which an opera company's budget is based. Its fixed costs – musicians, technicians, administrators, the building – are set in stone. Almost all income lines in the budget needed to pay for these fixed costs are estimates subject to events and at medium- to high-risk. From box-office income to forecasts of the sales for each production, to sponsorship and development, to secondary income such as hospitality, every line is an estimate, an educated guess. If each line was 'tweaked' up by 2 or 3 per cent, the income might meet the fixed costs and the budget might look as if it balanced. But who was to say if such usually upward 'tweaks' were justified or merely convenient for management? If the actual financial out-turn was worse than the over-optimistic predictions, then a deficit was inevitable. The margin between comparative success and reported failure was Micawber-like in its narrowness. Could the board ask just those questions about marginal calls without appearing to trespass on artistic responsibility?

This dilemma was felt most acutely by Richard Aikens, a leading QC and later judge, whose legal opinion was regularly canvassed as to whether ENO was trading insolvently: 'There is inevitably a conflict in questioning these assumptions or forecasts. They are after all essentially "padding items". Questioning them in the budget seemed to topple over into artistic interference. Yet the Board's duty was to ensure there was enough financial control and to persuade the Chief Executive they didn't have the money for everything they wanted to do. But the mildest attempts to question these numbers were greeted with the response that "You're not a professional". To this day, Aikens regrets not being more robust about the numbers: 'Instead of saying, "We can just about do it", we would have had to set a different course.'

If this made the board's fundamental responsibility of supervision hard (or even impossible) to execute, Aikens lays the charge of failure at their door: 'The Board was not honest enough to challenge the budget assumptions. We did not confront the General Director with his over optimism about the numbers.' This is a charge strongly contested by John Baker, but a later company executive observed: 'I was very confused as to how so many smart people could be in the dark about how serious the financial problems were.'

Increasingly, as ENO struggled to reconcile budgets with artistic realities and the minutiae of ACE funding criteria and settlements, John Baker as chairman found an increasing number of weaknesses in Dennis Marks' grip on management and the numbers. When a deal was agreed to buy out so-called 'Spanish practices' – i.e. traditional inefficiencies or downright abuses – among stage hands and technicians, Baker observed barely half of the supposed efficiency gains were ever delivered. What was management doing? When a £1 million loan was provided for a programme of redundancies and ENO's overall deficit rose to £4 million, Baker started walking around the building and talking to staff to see what was going on for himself. After confronting the general director with what he had found, Marks tried to ban Baker from entering the Coliseum without his permission. The breakdown of trust was complete, the writing on the wall.

It had been a long time coming. Even a good friend like Rodric Braithwaite observed: 'There will always be tension between the artistic and financial side in an opera company. But things will go wrong if the two sides are not open with one another. Dennis tried to bamboozle the Board with assurances that turned out to be froth.' Baker lamented the 'wrestling matches' at awaydays at Harewood and later Sarsden, where Marks laid out his operatic plans and 'never, never said how he would deliver them!' He concluded that Dennis was very bad at transparency: 'His whole policy was to deny the Board information to the maximum possible extent. Part of my serious discussions with him were on the lines of "up with this I will not put".' Sally Groves insists Marks was never even subconsciously putting Peter Jonas' cynical advice into practice but the end result of his actions was much the same. My own view is that a lifetime of shouldering financial responsibility in programme production at the BBC made him incapable of sharing what he knew.

On Dennis Marks' side, he felt Baker was not ready to stand up for what he thought was right. According to Sally Groves, he felt himself 'sinking into a morass of half-truths and compromises' with ACE not giving ENO the money it needed: 'He would have compromised on some things but he felt ACE would not see there was no way of squaring the circle financially and he felt the dishonesty deeply.'

Twenty years on, ironically, Baker and Marks are agreed on one thing. According to Sally Groves, 'All through the last year he said, "I should have walked after the first year." He would have felt his reputation and record was clear.' Today, John Baker says, 'I knew after 18 months that Dennis would not be able to reconcile what he wanted to do with what was available. He set his face against trimming.' His vision was all. Baker recalls that once or twice he suggested to the board that Marks 'should go early. But there was no Board enthusiasm for that at all.' The delay helped nobody, especially Marks. 'When he did go,' says Sally Groves, 'it was not nice. Nothing like this had happened to him before.'

It may be the only thing a board can do but getting rid of a chief executive is a heavy deed. Ever since, I have wondered if the board could have handled Dennis Marks differently, more fairly, whether we might perhaps have saved him from himself. Tony Cleaver looks back with a feeling of sadness but inevitability: 'There probably had to be a change.' Rodric Braithwaite wishes, 'the Board could have managed him better. If the Board had acted sooner, he might have been saved. But he would have had to take a more realistic and open view of the finances. I am not sure he was capable of that.' Bob Boas notes bleakly: 'The Board can't change the character of a chief executive.' That is why the original choice of one is so crucial – there is only a single chance to get it right, then only a single and brutal way to act when it goes wrong.

During the last 18 months of Dennis Marks' tenure as general director, my home diary has several references to 'supper with Dennis and

Sally'. They were suppers 'à quatre' at our house with only one topic of conversation: the situation at the Coliseum and what Dennis might or could do to resolve the conflict between what he wanted to do and what he felt the board and Arts Council would let him do. I cannot recall what advice – if any – I offered. Outside in the gloaming of the garden, our wives, Ann Tusa and Sally Groves, had parallel conversations. The agony and the impossibility of compromise would have been in the air in both groups. Each choice was hard to contemplate. At one of the board awaydays at his elegant country mansion of Sarsden in Oxfordshire, Shaun Woodward and I sat up late with Dennis, trying to help him to face a choice of unpleasant facts. He was wracked and it was awful to see a friend's anguish. Those who think the comings and goings in arts organizations are a series of formal conventions of a privileged world without feelings or painful consequences have never witnessed one as it unfolds.

In due course, with dismissal decided as inevitable, John Baker and Charles Alexander called on Lord Gowrie, Chairman of the Arts Council. They warned him of their impending action. Gowrie replied: 'This is a timely discussion. Without Marks going, we are out of this venture.' At least that was unambiguous but the entire way the ACE exercised its power and control over ENO, in many ways rendering the board's decisions nugatory and raising questions about the workings of good governance itself, has still to be discussed. As this chapter of ENO's troubled history closed, the final thoughts of Dennis Marks ring clear from his wife Sally Groves: 'When he resigned, Dennis said ENO would be back "in shtuck" within four years. They were there in two. The Arts Council were to blame.' His career never recovered.

Dennis Marks resigned as General Director of English National Opera on 16 September 1997. His departure failed to solve ENO's problems, it merely marked the next chapter of crises at the Coliseum. Once again, they turned on and were shaped by relations between the chairman and the general director. Would we as a board do better in choosing the right blend, of achieving 'partnership and separation' the second time round?

The first task was to choose a successor to Marks. By the end of the year, the board was looking at a decent set of candidates with the field narrowing to two with strong credentials: Nicholas Payne from the Royal Opera and Richard Jarman from Scottish Opera. Today, at least three members of the selection committee recall their support for Jarman. If he was unshowy and personally self-effacing, with a track record at Scottish Opera and a brief stint shoring up the then teetering administration at the Royal Opera, Jarman was 'a safe pair of hands'. Exciting, no, practical, yes. By contrast, Nicholas Payne had a record of mounting exciting seasons of opera at Opera North and Covent Garden. Once John Baker had received assurances about Payne's readiness to manage budgets, he and others saw two factors working strongly in his favour: Payne was the operatic visionary, Jarman the practical administrator. Further, ENO's Music Director, Paul Daniel, had formed a successful team with Nicholas Payne at Opera North. Why not re-establish it and play to proven success? As Baker saw it, Daniel had been playing a public leadership role in keeping the company stable during Marks' turbulent final months and he needed to be listened to: 'The last thing we needed was to bring in a new general director and find that Paul Daniel was off.'

These were powerful and practical arguments. In retrospect, they are strange. English National Opera was in the midst of a crisis of finance, management and administration with awful relations with the principal funder, the Arts Council. These were the practical aspects that desperately needed putting right. By contrast, there was no comparable artistic crisis. ENO was mounting persuasive and successful productions on a regular basis. Artistically, it was not an impaired organization. To this day, Tom Chandos regards the choice of Nicholas Payne as a 'perverse appointment'.

There was nothing wrong with him but ENO's needs were different from what he had to offer and would bring. It might indeed seem perverse that a board of so-called 'suits' should have chosen the 'man of vision' over the 'man of affairs'. That is the way of boards: the rush of the exciting is better than the trudge of the sensible. And who wants to be associated with a board that takes the practical but boring decisions?

Like Marks, Payne found that the complex task of running an opera company in the last decade of the twentieth century was overlaid by two major distractions: relations with the Arts Council and the condition of the Coliseum. Marks' departure resolved neither. As if the earlier Stevenson inquiry into relations between the Royal Opera and English National had not been disruptive enough, albeit ineffective, in November 1998, theatre director Richard Eyre was commissioned to report on the possible merger of the two companies working in a single venue at Covent Garden. The New Labour government was reported to be in fighting mood: 'We need hard decisions and need to be unpopular.' Baker spotted the government's game: 'that the Royal Opera should become a receiving house and so that we could perform there and lose our identity'. It had to be fought. Six months later, Chandos recalled how publication did huge damage to ENO; he cites its opening paragraph as saying, 'the Royal Opera House is international; English National Opera sings in English.' Could anything be more diminishing and patronizing of ENO? Yet it could have been far worse. Eyre's report totally threw out the 'one house' suggestion and added that the arts needed more money from the government, not less. Baker noted with grim satisfaction: 'We turned him.' In truth, Richard Eyre was too much of a man of the theatre to have believed that two established and creative performing companies could just be shoehorned by government diktat into a single building.

The real lesson from the incessant, opportunistic and finally futile string of government-induced inquiries into arts provision in the 1990s was that it was government and not the Arts Council that pulled the strings of national art policy. In shredding the lauded 'keeping at arm's length' principle and directing the Arts Council, this also undermined the basic rule and practices of good board governance. The implications for each institution should have been profound. But the condition of the Coliseum itself could no longer be ignored. A total refit of the building as it stood had been ruled out; the possibility of a 'new build' alongside Tower Bridge torpedoed. The remaining option, a real practical imperative, was a 'restoration' of the building but only of the public spaces front of house. Given that this works programme would not, and could not, remedy the wholly unsuitable realities backstage, where a tightly landlocked site lacked space for incoming productions, it is remarkable that such a compromise project ever found favour and support. The fact is there was no alternative: the Coliseum was falling apart.

The restoration announcement in March 2001 put a brave face on it. Nothing had been done to the theatre since it was built almost a century before. It would be restored to its original glory on its centenary birthday in 2004. At a projected cost of £41 million, it would add 40 per cent to the audience space and 'experience' front of house. Two further statements were highly questionable, if not downright misleading. The first that there would be 'improved facilities backstage', the second that there would be 'minimum disruption to the company's operations as Britain's only full-time opera repertory company'. Both would prove disastrously inaccurate and inflict real damage on the company's financial stability.

If running an opera company during partial closure of its permanent home was a major headache for Nicholas Payne, worse came with the appointment of the new chairman of the board, Martin Smith. Some in the opera-loving community had wondered how John Baker, whom they pigeon-holed patronizingly in the category of 'businessman', could have the temperament and understanding to chair an opera board. By these standards, Baker's successor, Martin Smith, looked far, far worse, being a banker. Arguably, the board chose him for the wrong reasons. He would give £1 million personally to the restoration appeal; he would head the appeal; he would deliver it because, as the saying goes, 'only someone who has given can ask others to give'. That is the iron rule of fundraising. The board judged it essential to demonstrate leadership in giving from its head. We were lucky, it was said, to have a person with such 'high net worth' to commit to our rescue. A few wondered whether chairman of the Development Appeal would not have been a more suitable role for Smith. He made it clear that chairmanship of the main board was essential for his support. The board accepted while knowing in truth very little about the person we had just invited to direct our affairs. A few felt totally excluded from the discussions surrounding the appointment, which they felt was done by an 'inner circle' of trustees.

Four years later, the £41 million restoration was delivered 'on time and on cost'. It was in its own limited terms a brilliant success. Martin Smith had been tireless in raising the needed funds, that cannot be taken away. The real hero of the project was the property expert, Christopher Jonas (no relation to former director Peter Jonas). Christopher chaired the project board with ruthless control. I once asked him how he kept contractors' costs under control. 'It was very simple,' he explained. 'When a contractor came to you, saying some part of the work was going to turn out more expensive, I would say, "Did you sign the contract for this sum?" Yes. "Is this your signature on the contract?" Yes. "Well then, I think that is your problem." And they usually went away.' It needed vast knowledge and experience of the property business, a steely mind and a poker face, all of which Christopher Jonas possessed. His almost single-handed achievement, a solitary bright light in the darkening world of the fortunes of English National Opera at the time, deserves special recognition.

Long before that date, we on the ENO Board were finding that the
choice of Martin Smith as chairman was problematic, generous financially
as he was. As Tony Cleaver put it bluntly: 'Bankers aren't managers.' Tom
Chandos saw him as the prisoner of his own prejudices, arriving with
the belief common to business people that common sense can solve
most problems. He thought there were 'easy pickings, lots of low-lying
fruit to be got from increasing efficiency' at ENO. What Smith did not
understand, argues Chandos, was that 'not-for-profits are much better
run than they appear. Miracles are worked year on year, even if budgets
weren't balanced as often as they should have been.' Such perspectives of
wisdom and modesty were largely absent from Smith's outlook because
they were so remote from his own experience.

Martin Smith committed one major personal error: with his bow ties
and flamboyant manner, he looked both 'rich and arrogant' and gave the
impression that he saw himself as the public representative of English
National Opera; he thought that he was 'the story' of ENO. In doing so, he
broke the first rule in the chairman's rulebook and became the lightning
conductor for public controversy and press criticism. John Baker told me
how he once took him aside and said, '"Martin, that's not the way to do
it," but he didn't really want to know.' He made himself an easy target. The
media was only too happy to take aim.

Given the amount of media coverage he attracted, also his sensitivity to
public commentary, Tom Chandos judged that Smith's characteristics of
'self-confidence, arrogance and a thin skin were a difficult combination.'
And so it proved. For Richard Aikens, Smith was a martinet, 'utterly
the wrong person to run an arts board, a banker who thought only in
plus and minus signs, lacking any understanding of how to manage the
executive of an arts organization.' This was the person who was supposed
to work constructively, 'in partnership but with separation', with a general
director with a strong record of achievement, widely admired in the

opera world, high confidence in his abilities and an arrogance to match that of his chairman.

Clash of personalities apart, the Smith/Payne combination was dealt a difficult hand. The financial costs of having to take so many productions out of the Coliseum because of closures for restoration were high. Payne himself proved surprisingly fallible – if unapologetic – in his choice of directors of what should have been standard repertoire. These lost audiences, money and reputation. Meanwhile, the glamorously restored Royal Opera was winning hearts, minds, critics and audiences. But the Smith/Payne combination was not a team, they were divided by a huge rift of approach. Tom Chandos recalls saying to Nicholas at an early board event: 'The Board is not against risk but we want to know what risks are being taken rather than how they can be buried.' Payne, Chandos recalls, looked puzzled: 'He thought board members at all institutions were pretty philistine and repressive of artistic creativity. The less you told them, the greater the chance you had of doing good work.' Transparency in information, trustworthiness in behaviour were at risk.

Martin Smith, whatever his outward and temperamental shortcomings, was no fool over money. Nor, says Charles Alexander, was he unreasonable or wrong in his scrutiny: 'He was never satisfied with the presentation of the funds or of how he wanted them presented. He felt that the actual numbers were always playing catch-up with the art.' What he looked for was 'This is what we have, this is what we expect, make it work'. Even if the expectation was expressed clumsily, it was not an unreasonable demand for a chairman to make of his chief executive. And Smith's analysis of ENO's underlying problems was, in Alexander's view, correct: 'He lifted the stone from the truth. If you take stabilization funds from ACE, you should use them to set the company to the right size. But if stabilisation is taken as an addition to core funding, you will always operate at a deficit.' Rodric Braithwaite observed: 'There was always a tension between "vision" and "management". Martin tried to get the budget under control but he did it too brutally.' And he believes Smith was 'unjustly abused' by the media and the musical 'luvvies' for trying to get a grip on the money. They might know about opera performance but were wholly ignorant of what was involved in running an opera company.

In one sense only Smith and Payne were well-matched: each was supremely confident in his own abilities, each took a dim view of the abilities of others. The board was paying the price for two flawed appointments; for choosing vision over practicality, for choosing fundraising over chairmanship. In the process we put together an ill-matched top leadership for ENO. Add to the clash of minds and temperaments the complex brew of artistic weakness, box-office shortfalls, over-conservative repertoire planning and the costs of not performing at the Coliseum and a second departure of an ENO general director was bound to come. Nicholas Payne left in July 2002. The public opprobrium for losing a highly respected figure in the opera world was intense. It fell mainly on the chairman, Martin Smith. He found that if as chairman of an organization you make yourself the story, you pay the price.

The Board then failed in its main responsibility, that of appointing a further chief executive. We chose Sean Doran, a festival director with no experience of running a company of any kind, let alone an opera house. We did him no favours. I sat on the committee searching for the new general director. Shell-shocked by almost a decade of turmoil, we felt we had to fill the leadership vacuum and do so expeditiously. We were ridiculed for it. The board broke the first rule of making appointments: 'If you can't see the right candidate in front of you, don't appoint'. It was a lesson hard learned.

Doran never looked likely to solve any of ENO's problems. With another departure firmly on the board's agenda, I had a meeting with

Martin Smith. I got on well with him and liked his raffish charm. Over lunch, I said: 'Look, Martin, any board can part with one chief executive. Some boards have to part with two. No board can lose three. We have to go.' Doran resigned in November 2005, Smith followed less than a month later, bitter and unreconciled. At a farewell dinner organized by Vernon Ellis, his successor, and his wife Hazel, at their Kensington home, Martin broke down in tears.

Two questions arise from the turbulent decade in which I sat on the ENO Board. Was the board's failure to shape events effectively a reflection of its failure to think and act strategically? Throughout the 1990s and beyond, English National Opera was beset by at least eight problems, which all impinged on its nature, purpose and identity.

Should it continue to perform as a repertory opera in a building totally unsuited to its needs? Was it truly a company of settled, contracted performers or was this a sentimental throwback to former times? Should it continue to sing in English when elsewhere, the operatic world was singing in the language in which the opera was written? Should it follow everyone else and introduce supertitles, or was this, too, a betrayal of the original mission? Come to that, what was ENO's 'mission' in the twenty-first century and was it enough to invoke the spirit of its founder, Lilian Baylis? What was its position vis-à-vis the glamorous forces of the Royal Opera just around the corner, or were we just 'London's second house?' Was ENO the anti-elitist house or was this a cosy delusion because all opera-goers are automatically classed as elitist?

Addressing these matters together could at least have given ENO a clear profile and an impression of a strong settled public and social purpose. A strategic approach to the portfolio of issues would have set about wrapping them up in a comprehensive settlement. Of course, the board wouldn't have solved every problem all at once or even in the same time frame, but demonstrating that we had an awareness of total needs, a systematic and coherent approach to them, a strategy for change to a bundle of problems might have strengthened ENO's public standing. That approach was never followed.

Some including Sir Vernon Ellis, chairman from 2006–12, insist that each of these issues was indeed faced by the board and some, such as the use of supertitles, were decided. This misses the point. Because they were considered from time to time, one by one, taken piecemeal, and never identified, presented and considered as a strategic whole, ENO always appeared beset by unfinished business, as indeed it was. As a result, it was critically nibbled to death, issue by issue, in what was seen as a welter of indecisiveness. For this, the board must take responsibility. Whether the music press had the skills to conduct such interrogation is beside the point. Theirs are the opinions and judgements that the music-going public read.

Why, as I believe, did the board fail to take on the big picture? Why was it so weak on strategy? Much of the time the location question, fraught as it was, became a substitute for strategy. Chandos thinks we were too busy firefighting and lacked a process for undertaking strategic reviews. Aikens believes the board never took a step back to think about what were ENO's coherent reasons for existence. Braithwaite judges the board to have been 'muddle-headed; we told ourselves stories about the "much-loved Coliseum". And clearly believed our own fairy stories. More fundamentally, he concludes: 'We couldn't reconcile imagination with arithmetic.' Alexander too recalls the board being so obsessed with numbers that 'we never discussed in much detail "What does success look like?"' That might have provoked proper strategic reflection.

There was an alternative model for ENO to adopt, according to Rodric Braithwaite, whose father had been a conductor for the famous theatrical producer Lilian Baylis: it was that of the 'second house' in Volksoper Wien in Vienna, or Komische Oper in Berlin. Both worked in the national language with younger singers and for a wider audience. Charles Alexander reflects that a real strategy for ENO could have involved the following elements: merger with English National Ballet (similar to Covent Garden); contract with a major London orchestra (like Glyndebourne); a freelance chorus; a talent development centre for music, theatre and dance (analogous to a conservatoire or the National Opera studio). But no such thoughts, ideas or possibilities were faced or considered even – or especially – in the beguiling settings of country house board 'awaydays' at Harewood, or Sarsden in Gloucestershire. To those who object that boards are not equipped for strategic thinking, the question might be, why not? There were plenty of 'mission statements' but little real strategy.

No assessment of the ENO Board's record in the 1990s can pass without analysis of the actions and policies of the public funder, Arts Council of England. It goes to the heart of governance principles. As funder of first and last resort, ACE wielded influence much of the time, power some of the time. Yet the accepted conventions of public funding in the United Kingdom were based on the principle of 'arm's length' distance from government. Since government increasingly pointed ACE in the directions it wished to be pursued, this principle was severely eroded. John Baker regarded 'arm's length' as 'only honoured in the breach. In the end, even if you got them onside, they wouldn't give.'

So, what did this do to the practices of governance which the board tried to observe? At every board meeting, each member knew that collectively, we held the business of ENO in legal trust. At one end of the table sat the 'ACE observer' bound by no such burdens or responsibilities. After each meeting, the 'observer' retired without a word to ACE headquarters, where far-reaching decisions were often taken about ENO's future. Certainly, Arts Council England were custodians of public money. This carried its own responsibilities of public accountability. But if these took precedence over the legal obligations of board governance, it made nonsense of the board's fiduciary responsibilities.

As Charles Alexander put it, 'There was a disconnect between the board and its governance and the complex governance of the institutions of government funding.' Within Whitehall, arts funding went through no fewer than four levels of decision-making: ENO Board, Arts Council, Office of Arts and Libraries and the Treasury. The board was the weakest, the supplicant, the Treasury, the most powerful. Yet communication operated as a paper chain of information and negotiation, of 'reported speech of reported speech', obfuscation not transparency. Major funding and policy decisions over strategies came down to a Whitehall version of 'Chinese whispers', where the final message mangled the original instruction. The results should have surprised no one.

Such matters were never acknowledged or resolved. Did the ACE exercise 'power without responsibility'? Former executive director Russell Willis Taylor prefers 'ideology without practicality'. She is immensely critical of the Council's basic competence in carrying out its responsibilities: 'The stabilisation programme was as badly run as any programme I ever encountered in my career. They wasted extraordinary sums of money on advice from a large accountancy firm, which had no idea of the nature of our business.' Coming from arguably ENO's most effective administrator in years, this is damning.

A decade and a half on, the board's feeling about the Arts Council's behaviour runs high and strong. John Baker regards three of their decisions as seriously damaging to ENO: the Stevenson Report, the Eyre Report and what he still regards as the 'betrayal' over ENO's proposed new home. Worse still, 'in my eight years as chairman, the handshake I had with ACE on four packages of stabilisation and restructuring, in every case they were not fully delivered, cut from £500K to £300K.' Russell Taylor observes drily: 'ACE were often on the defensive and the difference between what they said and what they did was marked.' Baker concludes: 'I am convinced the ACE agenda was always to reduce support for ENO.' Yet such crucial decisions, still less the thinking behind them, were never available for scrutiny or discussion at the board. How could openness in decision-making take place without?

Rodric Braithwaite offers a slight demurral: 'The ACE's pressure on us to act was in a way convenient for us. But the board should have been able to handle problems without needing to be put under external pressure. To ask the ACE to do the job that the board can't do – i.e. sack the CEO – is to ask a lot.'

I recall one meeting towards the end of my time in 2003 when an outright board rebellion might have occurred. The board faced an ACE funding proposal which left us a full £1 million short of what was needed to deliver the mission and the repertoire. Richard Aikens regarded the relationship between ENO and ACE as quite the worst aspect of the governance relationship: it was a one-sided relationship, a 'recipe for disaster'. On this occasion, he and I both said: 'Face them off, tell them it can't be done.' For good measure, Aikens suggested: 'Ask ACE, do you want ENO as a proper opera company or do you want something on the cheap?' That would have been a true challenge. That would have raised the strategic questions. The board was not up for the fight. What if it had been? To this day, I regret that we did not take that opportunity to flush out the evasions, the compromises, the pretences, the contradictions, the weasel-words that infected national arts policy. We were ships passing in the night and we went on our way into the darkness.

At the end of one of my conversations, I observed bleakly that all that was wrong with English National Opera had been 'wrong company, wrong home, wrong language'. No wonder the board could not save it. More bleakly still, 'The board failed, the chief executive failed, the chairman failed'. That is undoubtedly too harsh, too sweeping, too unfair to many. It can hardly be denied that governance did fail on key occasions but many others were complicit in its failure. The eighteenth-century French diplomat Talleyrand was asked what he had done during the French Revolution. He replied: 'I survived!' Like Talleyrand, English National Opera survived its crises to fight another day. That should not be underestimated. For what the board did throughout a turbulent decade deserves some credit. Besides, in the words of merchant banker Bob Boas, 'running an opera company is far harder than running a business'. All of us involved in the affairs of English National Opera during the decade discovered that the hard way.

REFLECTIONS

Chairman and chief executive should not be cut from the same cloth, but they should trust one another and be able to work together.

Boards should not appoint a chairman with no experience or understanding of chairmanship.

They should not appoint a chairman just because they can give and raise money: a fundraiser is a fundraiser.

Boards must be watchful over who they appoint and judge realistically if the chairman and chief executive fit.

The chairman of a not-for-profit should understand that creating social good is the reason for its existence, not the making of profit.

Boards should ensure the chief executive they appoint can address the immediate needs of the organization.

There is a time for a bold vision and a time for common sense.

A board should not appoint a chief executive who holds the board in contempt or is reluctant to be held to account.

Boards should not duck taking safe decisions even if the outside world thinks it is being feeble.

Business people who sit on arts boards are important and invaluable. They should never overlook the fact that not-for-profit boards are not worse than commercial boards, but they are different.

Boards hate not making appointments. Delay is the best course of action if there are doubts as to the suitability of a candidate. Six months' delay often produces a very different field of candidates.

'Suits are suits and luvvies are luvvies'. In practice, they have more in common than divides them.

Boards should question budget numbers even if that risks trespassing on artistic judgements.

'A board appoints and a board dismisses'. Is that an adequate response to the complex needs of contemporary governance?

If the government is abusing the principle of the 'arm's length policy', ministers should be challenged in the interests of the organization.

Reliance on private funding as in the United States is filled with problems, but government funding is equally problematic.

If the principle public funder is the effective decision maker about an organization's future, it should be liable to scrutiny within the parameters of governance.

The role of a funder and regulator like Arts Council England should be accommodated within the existing structures of governance.

Which is the more accurate description of ACE behaviour: 'Power without responsibility' or 'Ideology without practicality'? How long can it last?

Board members need to give even more of their time to understanding complex arts organizations.

However demanding, boards should raise their eyes from the detailed and practical and take the long look at strategy.

Property development is not in itself a strategy, though it has elements of strategy in it.

A board member wears four hats: the charity trustee with legal responsibilities, strategic oversight and sustainability, functional expertise, volunteering and ambassadorship on behalf of the organization.

Managing an opera company is far more difficult and complex than running a similar-sized or slightly larger business.

The days of being asked to join a board over tea at the Athenaeum are over!

4

The British Museum: 'A Most August and Ancient Board' (2000–2009)

Interviews with

Robert Anderson, Director, British Museum (BM)

Dawn Austwick, Deputy Director, BM

Sir John Boyd, Master, Churchill College, Cambridge; Chairman and BM Trustee

Lord Browne, CEO British Petroleum (BP); Trustee

Lord Broers, former Vice-Chancellor, Cambridge University; Trustee

Dame Liz Forgan, former Chair, Heritage Lottery Fund (HLF); Trustee

Niall FitzGerald, Chairman, Reuters; Chairman and BM Trustee

Baroness Helena Kennedy, Principal, Mansfield College, Oxford; Trustee

David Lindsell, partner, Ernst & Young; Trustee

Sir David Norgrove, Chairman, UK Statistics Authority; former Director Marks & Spencer; Trustee

Neil MacGregor, Director, BM

I had been managing director of the Barbican Centre for five years when I received an invitation from the Chairman of the British Museum, Graham Greene, to have lunch at the Garrick Club on 10 February 2000. We knew one another slightly, but our two institutions – the barely 20-year-old Barbican and the almost 250-year-old British Museum – could not have been further apart. Whatever the lunch was about, it was not cooperation between the institutions. I discovered its purpose only over coffee, the then traditional way of doing business in London's clubland. Would I like to become a trustee of the British Museum? I knew the Museum and visited the Department of Prints and Drawings frequently, but any real knowledge of the needs, purposes and business of the British Museum – always known as the 'BM' – was distant. All that seemed to matter was that such an invitation was an honour. Only a fool would have turned it down. I had no reason to do so and accepted.

I discovered later that Graham Greene had taken a political risk in inviting me to join, one of just five trustees in the direct gift of the BM Board. A further 15 were appointed by the government; four were nominated by the 'learned societies' such as the British Academy, one by HM The Queen herself. When Greene informed others that he was considering inviting me to join the board, colleagues warned, 'Don't do that, the Government doesn't like him.' (I had been too publicly critical of government arts policies). Greene's face lit up with a wolfish grin: 'That is a very good reason for having him.' I loved him for that. Day-to-day politics, as I soon found out, were never far away from this august, distinguished and historic institution.

The Museum was set up under an Act of Parliament in 1753. This coloured the trustees' responsibilities to 'hold the collections in trust for the nation' with a mantle of independence, public responsibility and a certain status of being exceptional. Few ever attended their first board meeting without experiencing a sense of awe at its size, the academic distinction of many of its members and the public standing of others. As one trustee put it, 'I was rather bemused as I looked around the table. I could see the point of most of the people there. There were very rich people. There were very political people, there were the very scholarly and I said to the Chairman, "Who am I?"' For the Royal Academician artist, Tom Phillips, entering the BM's boardroom was like 'a convocation of the Knights Extraordinary of the Long Rectangle, a huge table which stretched from end to end.' So long was the table, so poor the board room's acoustics, that, he recalled, 'deaf trustees would hasten to plant their papers near the centre in the vicinity of the Chairman.'

Even distinguished academics were puzzled as to what their role could be. A former Vice-Chancellor of Cambridge University, Alec Broers, remained puzzled by his presence. As a computer expert he knew about technology, but, as he put it, he had 'not been in the world of museums and I am rather naughty about history. I deal with the present and the present forwards is my sphere. I felt I would be a misfit.' How could his particular expertise serve the BM's needs? Another regular attendee believed the trustees gave the impression of being appointed less to serve than 'because they deserved something for having done something else'. They appeared to feel 'entitled'. A senior member of staff and observer of trustee meetings noted: 'It was straight out of the eighteenth century. The mace sat on the boardroom table. Once, when the Chairman seated himself in the chair facing it, he was told "Don't sit there, that is the Duke of Gloucester's seat [the Queen's appointment on the board], even if he isn't here."'

The BM's procedures throughout the 1990s were very quaint – and certainly had been for far longer than that. Trustees met nine times a year on a Saturday morning, a demanding schedule by other board standards. Some enjoyed the gentle atmosphere of these occasions, one was said to have remarked, 'You can talk about lots of things including the Museum's cats.' Each meeting began with a presentation of objects which the Museum's senior academic staff, the keepers, hoped to acquire. Trustees would advise how the BM's minuscule budget for acquisitions should be allocated. This activity was highly valued by many trustees, believing it kept them in close touch with both senior staff and the Museum's objects. Weren't they responsible for holding them in 'trust for the nation'? But another described it as 'a very scholarly car boot sale', with trustees playing the fantasy role of great collectors in the mould of the Museum's founder, Sir John Soane. 'Were we travellers in the eighteenth century,' pondered John Browne, 'looking at what people might sell us? It felt almost colonial'. If this was harmless as a board activity, it was soon to become a distraction, a displacement activity from the new, strenuous and, for some, alien demands of modern governance.

When I joined in July 2000, I was struck not just by the number of people on the board but by an avalanche of papers, sometimes arriving in two or more updated versions, and the three-hour-long meetings on Saturdays. There were two possibly mitigating factors: the table at the entrance to the boardroom was loaded with the latest publications from the BM Press, often wonderfully illustrated catalogues or learned records of archaeological research. Trustees were invited to take their unlimited pick of this cornucopia. As he filled two carrier bags with books, one observed, 'That's my Christmas present problem settled!'

The other particular pleasure, almost a diversion, was to find myself often seated next to Royal Academician Tom Phillips. His way of keeping concentration throughout long meetings was to doodle on the board papers. 'Doodle' is a wholly inadequate word to describe the intricately worked drawings that overlay the formal notifications of board business.

They may have helped Tom to concentrate but watching him 'doodling' was a dangerous if pleasurable distraction for me. (He later made a book out of them, *Merry Meetings*, as well as an art installation. The visual counterpoint of printed board agendas and his intricate workings deserved research.)

In those early days, I witnessed a further convention which also spoke of 'olden times' and a remote past. Slipping out of one meeting well past its scheduled 1 p.m. close, I went for a quick buffet lunch to catch up with senior staff, who were always expected to be 'in attendance'. Half a dozen distinguished scholars and administrators stood there, without food, without drink, the clingfilm wrap stretched tight over the dishes. Why were they not eating, I wondered. 'We can't start until the Chairman arrives,' was the reply. We ripped off the wrapping, opened the wine and got going. The chairman did not arrive for a full further 20 minutes.

It took longer to unwrap the Saturday morning meeting convention. A former and distant Archbishop of Canterbury, when asked what would fit His Grace's schedule for trustee meetings, replied that Saturday morning would suit very well as he could then write his Sunday sermon at Lambeth Palace in the afternoon. That long-distant Archbishop's personal convenience had hardened into an unexamined convention as if it too was part of the founding Act of Parliament.

I usually returned home by mid-afternoon on the Saturdays in question. My wife, Ann, then received a full 60-minute debriefing. I have always regretted not keeping a detailed journal of those occasions. In truth, the headline problems the BM trustees faced in 2000 were stark enough and there were three. The major development of the Great Court, shortly to be opened by HM The Queen, was surrounded with controversy. Almost six months previously, trustees had been told that the 'South Portico' of the Great Court, a new architectural element in the internal fabric of the building, had been built out of the 'wrong stone'.

This was unfortunate. Next, the BM was running a £6 million deficit, against its government grant of just £35 million. This was unjustifiable. Finally, the trustees had sleepwalked into a fully-fledged governance crisis. The director, historically the unchallenged chief executive in all matters scholarly and managerially, had been stripped of his authority as the person who answered to the government administratively, the so-called Accounting Officer. This had been transferred to a new post of managing director. The BM thus had a joint leadership, a source of bitterness, confusion and division so long as it lasted. Duumvirates have seldom survived in history, this was reckless. A capital development, a financial deficit, a governance crisis, a hat-trick of problems ... For each situation, the trustees were solely responsible. How had they allowed them to happen? I needed to understand what had gone on before I joined the board.

In large part, the situation may have sprung from a sense of the BM's past and an unchallenged standing that derived from its history and sheer longevity. Those who led the Museum in the 1990s, distinguished as they were, hardly helped matters. The chairman, Lord Windlesham, was regarded by Whitehall as imperious and uncompromising, with a habit of instructing civil servants about what the Museum's financial needs were and not engaging in explanation, let alone discussion. The legendary director, David Wilson, also treated any such government attempts at scrutiny with contempt. The notion of accountability would have been treated with puzzlement. If such a thing did exist, it was surely in relation to the Museum's collections. On one occasion, pressed by Treasury officials for information about the BM's future plans, Wilson was reported to have gathered up his papers and left the room.

John Browne, then Chief Executive of BP, arriving on the board in the mid-1990s, was shocked at what seemed the prevailing strong belief that 'if we ran the place into the ground someone would save us. The BM was too grand to fail, too important to fail'. That was complacent. When Liz Forgan, Chair of the Heritage Lottery Fund, was invited to lunch to hear about a BM application for funding for the Great Court, 'They simply said, "We're the British Museum, we're very grand and important and we would now like several million pounds to build an education centre". Forgan recalls: 'When I asked them what it would mean for the institution, what they thought about education, nobody had the faintest idea. The Museum had lost its way.' That was a sense of entitlement; the BM got nothing.

Arrogance, complacency, entitlement, a deadly concoction just when the 'Whitehall managerial revolution' of the 1980s was sweeping through the arts and lapping at the columns and steps of the world's oldest national public museum. Neither trustees nor managers were prepared for or even aware of what was changing.

Fundamentally, the BM's governance model was unbalanced. It was based on an essential tripod. Relations between trustees, scholarship and management worked in a very particular way. Each trustee was assigned a museum department for their special interest and attention. The historian, Keith Thomas, strongly approved and valued this: 'You got to see the workings of one part of the Museum in great detail, in 3D, more than you would ever have got sitting at the trustees' table. I think that the staff liked it. Once it disappeared, the board was more remote.' In the view of the artist, Tom Phillips, the loss of this relationship amounted to a 'diminution of the trustees' role'. It was, in the opinion of Robert Anderson, director from 1992, a board well-suited to this purpose, 'a board which knew a lot about the collections, specialists in many cases, art historians, ethnographers, archaeologists.' On the other hand, with his business background, John Browne observed a very different result from this system. The BM at that point, he observed, was not a single institution: 'It was eleven museums. Each department had trustees associated with it, so trustees were aligned with the department, not actually with the museum.' A corollary was that it worked as a highly diffused leadership system of power, where individual keepers were favourites of particular trustees, who made things work in their interest.

The implications were profound. In Browne's judgement, the scholarly departments, the heart of the Museum's existence, had become baronies: 'They were reinforced by the structure of the Board, so the Trustees were, as it were, suborned into the actual structure of the museum.' Keepers in practice reported more to their departmental trustees than to the director. In doing so, perhaps driven by an admirable belief in the overriding value of scholarship, trustees fell into the trap of becoming involved in operations. The essential governance triangle of trustees/scholarship/management was out of kilter. In the early 1990s this model might have seemed the right one for a great world museum, but where did this leave management? Shockingly weak, as events would soon reveal.

Under these circumstances, when David Wilson retired as director in 1992, it must have seemed natural that one scholar director should be succeeded by another. Robert Anderson was seen as having done a good job in Edinburgh, where he successfully integrated the Royal Scottish Museum with the National Antiquities Museum to form the National Museums Scotland, the country's largest multi-disciplinary museum, and persuaded the Scottish Education Department to fund an entirely new building to house them. Highly recommended by David Wilson, the trustees felt they need look no further. Like Wilson, Anderson believed in the importance of the collections, the primacy of scholarly research, in serious academic exhibitions, in focussing museum effort in these directions and avoiding the populism towards which he thought the Science Museum in South Kensington, London, was drifting. It all added up to a natural fit with the way the BM was being run – trustees and scholars in close harmony, managers a very poor third.

At this point, the British Museum was given the opportunity of its whole existence. The centre of the BM site was occupied by the British Library, the legendary Round Reading Room filling the central courtyard like the centre of a doughnut. With the British government promising a new and separate building for the British Library (BL) at St Pancras, the BM had to find new uses for acres of space within its perimeter. On Anderson's arrival as director, he found preliminary plans which turned the Round Reading Room into museum storage and for good measure added four further storage towers at each corner of the courtyard. This seemed a wasted opportunity, bereft of imagination or vision, as it offered nothing for exhibitions, scholarship or the growing numbers of visitors. Working with the chairman, Lord Windlesham, Anderson drew up a fresh brief for the use of the inner courtyard, which identified a future 'Great Court' as a key feature to improve visitor circulation. Windlesham and Anderson also planned new purposes for the Round Reading Room and the King's Library. Once Norman Foster and Spencer de Grey's vision of a glass-roofed Great Court and a magnificently stone-clad Reading Room as its centrepiece appeared, the BM seemed on the road to a new and brilliant future. The academic and statistician Claus Moser became trustee Chair of the BM Development Trust, an exempt charitable trust. Possessed of unlimited charm, huge powers of persuasion, deploying calculated quantities of flattery, marshalling unrivalled contacts through Whitehall, the City and London society, Moser was the fundraiser par excellence. What could go wrong?

It was not Robert Anderson's fault that he was neither manager nor administrator; the trustees had appointed him as scholar-director. By the mid-1990s the job demanded qualities which were not met by his academic strengths. With the British Library moving out to St Pancras, the British Museum would lose more than £3 million involved in rents and maintaining the site and its security on behalf of the British Library. Not unreasonably, the BM felt that the Department for National Heritage should make good the shortfall. After all, moving the BL had been the government's decision, why should they pick up the tab?

The trustees then made what proved to be an historic error. In the hope of persuading the Treasury that they deserved to be recompensed for the costs of the British Library's departure, they commissioned Andrew Edwards, a former deputy secretary at the Treasury, to make their case for them. According to a BM staffer who supported Edwards' work, he was given little guidance as to the terms of reference for his report, though the trustees were certainly looking for a 'clean bill of health'. Whether they would ever have got one from a former Treasury official is very unlikely. Without a clear brief, Edwards seems to have taken matters into his own hands. His final report in October 1996 was titled ominously 'The British Museum: A Fundamental Review of the Museum's Operations'. Edwards' report considered the whole of management, from finance to the budget, pay, grading and security. Anything but a 'clean bill of health', it revealed what he saw as a catalogue of deficiencies: the BM had no finance director, it employed no qualified accountants, it aggregated spending on current and capital, it allowed staff numbers to grow while the budget for acquisitions fell, it regularly tried to keep control of the budget by arbitrary last-minute cuts, provided they did not affect staff. Far from being a clean bill of health, the report read like a charge sheet of managerial incompetence. It seemed to question why anyone should trust the Museum with money. Whitehall and the arts commentariat made hay.

Even a generally sympathetic writer like Andreas Whittam Smith in the *Independent*, who found several of Edwards' recommendations contradictory, noted the Museum was dealing with government cuts of 24 per cent in real terms. Critical as he might be of the British government's actions, he insisted that they must apply modern methods of financial management, control staffing and make real savings. But the cat was out of the bag. The BM, it seemed, could not manage its affairs; governance was not up to it. By contrast, other major galleries such as Tate and the National Gallery were powering ahead with modernized systems of administration, governance and project management without detriment to their artistic and cultural purposes. The BM looked badly out of step and out of line. Whitehall increasingly thought so.

To this day, the director, Robert Anderson, regards the trustees' decision to commission the Edwards report as 'a big mistake, a disaster for us'. The National Audit Office (NAO), he points out, had previously given the British Museum a 'clean bill of health' on its regular inspections. He accuses Edwards personally of lacking any understanding of the BM's mission, of actively colluding with the Permanent Secretary at the Department of Culture against them and of misrepresenting the financial position. Others may wonder at the trustees' naivety in assuming a civil servant outsider would be likely to find their management systems efficient and effective. Their lack of self-knowledge of the institution is as striking as was their inability to spot that the winds in Whitehall were now set strongly against them. Almost 250 years old, the BM would always be, in one sense, too grand to be allowed to fail. But the years of unquestioning or uncritical support were long over. With Whitehall primed for action, BM trustees then played into their hands. Two events in the following year made it easy.

Windlesham's term as chairman had come to an end in April 1996. The choice of chairman of the British Museum was in the hands of the trustees. Their preferred successor was an existing and longstanding trustee, the publisher Graham Greene. Unfortunately, Greene's term as one of the government-nominated trustees expired shortly before Windlesham's.

The British government declined to appoint him to a further term so that he could slip into the chairman's seat. Almost certainly, he was seen as too connected with the 'old ways' of governance, which government was now determined to change.

At this point, in what they probably saw as a neat manoeuvre, the trustees appointed Greene to a fresh term as one of the five trustees in their gift. As such, he immediately succeeded Windlesham in the chair. Whitehall was furious, but the trustees had acted well within their powers. Politically, they overplayed an already weak hand and were to do so once again.

Anderson's first five-year term as director had closed at the end of 1996. For many in the Museum and on the board, it should have done so. It was not simply that internal opinion had turned against him; keepers were urging trustees to 'sort things out' by changing the director. The range of demands increasingly put on museums had grown in complexity. In John Browne's assessment, the agenda facing the director now went well beyond scholarship and curation of collections. It included broadening the social demographic of visitors, mounting more varied exhibitions, earning more money and extending opening hours. All were essential in an era when government funding was falling and the functions of museums were developing. Anderson was seen as more and more behind the times. As Browne recalled, 'It wasn't Robert's fault that he didn't have the skills needed. He was never trained for it, to do all these things and get them in the right order.'

Anderson's eventual successor, Neil MacGregor, lays the responsibility for the position the British Museum found itself in squarely on the trustees: 'The duty of the Chair and board is surely to ensure that having appointed a director, the director has around him or her the skills required for the institution to run. No director is going to possess all the necessary skills.'

Whitehall saw no justification for renewing the tenure of a director whose management, as they saw it, had been so fundamentally exposed by the Edwards report. Greene and Moser, however, may have thought that any public disruption in the Museum's leadership would send the wrong signal about its stability during a critical time for fundraising for the Great Court. For his part, Anderson believes that the trustees' mood was still 'we are not going to be pushed around by DCMS [the Department for Digital, Culture, Media & Sport] in this kind of way'. They voted to renew him as director for five years from January 1997.

The trustees seem not to have appreciated, or perhaps not cared, that for the second time in a few months they had defied the government. Constitutionally, they had every right to do so. Given the BM's shredded reputation for competence, the growing budgetary problems, the reductions in public funding, the fact that the government was principal paymaster, such defiance was politically naive and disastrous. Whitehall got its revenge in its own way. Yes, Anderson could stay on as director if the trustees insisted, that was their right. But the government would no longer accept him as the person who reported to them on finance. He was duly stripped of his role as accounting officer. That was *its* right.

This was no arcane piece of Whitehall machination; the Permanent Secretary at the Department for Digital, Culture, Media & Sport was, after all, the Joint Accounting Officer for the British Museum's affairs. He had to have confidence in his partner. It was certainly a blow to the BM's reputation and standing. They had appointed a director with whom Whitehall would not deal financially. Very well, the trustees would have to find a figure who could run the Museum and who the DCMS would accept as their trusted interlocutor in Whitehall. They had to create a new position, a managing director. Whoever took the job would not be popular. Anderson does not recall being consulted about the change until it happened.

The trustees met to review the new post of managing director with accounting officer status. John Boyd, a former diplomat, suggested they should consider a woman. There was 'shock, horror around the room,' he recalls. But a woman it was to be.

When the headhunter Anthony Saxton approached Suzanna Taverne about applying for the job, he was very open about the task ahead. 'We're going to deploy the "slip of a girl" strategy,' he advised. 'One group of trustees will completely underestimate you and that's good. On that basis they'll take you. The other group of trustees, and they're the ones who matter, will understand they're getting someone who's up to the job.' Taverne herself saw the trustees split three ways. The first group said, 'The sacred flame [of authority] is still intact and Robert Anderson is in charge'. This was delusional. The second declared, 'This makes sense with the right skills for the manager of the organization and the right skills for curatorial leadership.' This was far too advanced. The third, perhaps led by John Browne, said, 'We think we have someone who can get this job done.' That was pragmatic.

In taking the new post of Managing Director, British Museum, Taverne herself thought the trustees had made a mistake in keeping Anderson as director and in dividing the leadership roles in this 'uncomfortable way'. But as she joined in May 1999, she recalls taking three bets with herself: first, that she could work amicably in a duumvirate with Robert Anderson, his authority as director publicly emasculated; second, that she could play her part in delivering the Great Court scheme; finally, that after proving her worth in that role, she could be seen as a plausible candidate for the actual directorship. All three were high-risk bets: one was improbable, one impossible. She joined nevertheless.

It was never going to be a happy relationship. Anderson was director in name, Taverne chief executive in title and in fact. Taverne maintains they had 'no public conflicts, no private conflicts.' She judged him to have been 'relieved not to have responsibilities other than being the public face and ambassador for the Museum. It included a lot of travelling abroad and he liked doing that.' He never interfered in the administration.

Anderson recalls his effective demotion very differently: 'It was terrible. It was huge pressure on me from all sorts of angles. I had to work with this woman who clearly wanted my job. I didn't like the way she was operating.'

The trustees were under no illusion about the consequences of their decision. Keith Thomas saw it as a 'statement of no confidence in the Director from the outside, maybe from the inside.' He assumed the chairman had yielded under pressure from the DCMS. Thomas recalled that Suzanna Taverne was not popular: 'She had been imposed. There was not an enthusiastic welcome for her, not a terribly warm atmosphere.' Tom Phillips recalls it as 'a muddle, two voices in disagreement.' Others, such as the Astronomer Royal Martin Rees, were harsher: 'The import of Suzanna Taverne was an insult to Robert. It proved to be a failure. Right from the start, she showed her lack of commitment by not cancelling a holiday to attend her first trustee meeting. She was just a "hired gun" with no serious commitment.' Fair or unfair, the result, says Rees, was tense for both and demoralizing for the director.

Two questions arise: why did Robert Anderson not resign when stripped of his accounting officer status? He says he never considered it, largely for very personal reasons: he needed to pay to educate his two children at boarding school and the official director's residence within the British Museum perimeter in the centre of London was no place to bring up a family. Besides, he had no alternative job in sight although he recalls 'one miserable lackey in DCMS saying there was a job at UNESCO I might be interested in.' Since it did not involve working with collections, his skill and his love, he turned it down.

The universal governance nostrum about relations between chairman and director is one of full backing until they have to be removed. The question for the trustees is why did they not part company with Anderson when his term expired? They would have had reasons aplenty to do so, including the Edwards report and the observable fact, according to John Browne, who liked him personally, that Anderson was 'out of his depth. The rate of change and the need to repair the BM's culture was just too much for him.' The era of the scholar/director was over. What had the trustees put in its place? A two-headed, warring hydra, the result of their own confusion, misjudgement of their standing and failure to realize that the world in which museums existed had altered beyond their recognition.

The future Director of the British Museum, Neil MacGregor, is scathing about their collective failure: 'The Trustees failed to recognize that if the Director is not accepted as Accounting Officer then he cannot do the job as Director. If he doesn't have the role and obligations of Accounting Officer, he doesn't have the authority inside the house to set policy, make decisions and balance academic and financial matters.' This judgement was not being wise after the event; when he became director, MacGregor worked to and applied this model.

If splitting the authority of leadership amounted to a serious failure of governance, the trustees legitimately face a further charge of lack of generosity towards the newly appointed Managing Director, Suzanna Taverne. She had not been foisted on them, though several felt she had been, but was in post as a direct result of their decisions. Her rather too open ambition to be considered a possible successor to Robert Anderson did not help, but it could never excuse the suppressed atmosphere of suspicion and hostility surrounding her actions. Besides, Taverne had been given a job to do by the trustees and the BM needed to have it done properly.

The year 1999 tested the new management and faltering governance to the limit. In the following 20 months, the BM was to take its first steps on the road to recovery, to control of its projects and to mending its self-respect. In March 1999, the trustees debated the issue of charging for entry to museums and galleries. The whole museum and gallery sector faced huge financial difficulties and determined pressure from government to introduce charging. Knowing the accumulated resentment at the Museum that had built up in Whitehall, this cannot have been a simple discussion, but the trustees behaved in a commendably defiant way while many other major institutions fell into the government's line. They insisted charging would be the last possible option. Claus Moser led the opposition and declared only two choices remained: either the BM should cut its activities or the grant-in-aid from the government should be increased. Since the latter was not going to happen, the trustees knew they were facing down the government yet again. There is something admirable in a stand on the principle of free entry regardless of financial or political consequences; it was the BM trustees of old at their independent and principled best. Whitehall never compensated those museums who 'stayed free' for any loss of revenue. The BM was not singled out for a petty revenge but must have deemed it worth suffering some financial loss for the self-respect earned from a principled stand.

There were the first signs that year that the museum was starting to modernize its administration. Suzanna Taverne introduced a new internal structure where she chaired all executive meetings. The atmosphere was more business-like. Two important board committees came under new leadership: Finance, under a new trustee, the accountant David Lindsell, and Audit, chaired by John Browne. The two men knew one another and sat in on each other's committees, creating a central core of substantial governance oversight over finance. This was just as well since the full board, according to Lindsell, was 'quite happy to delegate financial matters to these "business people!"'. The very presence of financial matters on the agenda seemed to be 'taking up their time!' Lindsell found the accounts to be 'a bit impenetrable and I said, what we need here is a "Rosetta Stone" to understand them!' They revealed a growing deficit so serious that Lindsell went directly to the DCMS to warn a minister that without increased funding, 'We're going to have to retrench and make cuts and I explained some of the areas where we would cut.' It is a sign of how unacceptable the language of 'cuts' and budgetary control was within the Museum that, rather than thank Lindsell for fighting with a minister for the BM, fellow trustees turned on him for contemplating cuts: 'I had one particularly vitriolic letter from a trustee saying that I really didn't know what I was talking about and all these reforms and change programmes were completely unnecessary. It was quite awful.' Another 'business' trustee, David Norgrove, once a director of the retailer Marks & Spencer, was roundly told by an academic trustee that he was the kind of person who would rip the historic bookcases out of libraries and replace them with plastic. Such were the teething pains of the modernization of governance, they verged on culture wars.

The high summer of 1999 proved a turning point as the Great Court development moved closer to being a reality. Undoubtedly, the architectural vision of Norman Foster and Spencer de Grey in creating a curving roof of 1,656 separately shaped glass panels had caught the public imagination. It beguiled with visions of the skies in all their formations, moods and colours. So had a variety of very public promises by the British Museum that the Great Court would be not just the heart of the museum but a 'new piazza' for London available out of museum hours and also providing a new public 'through way' from north to south Bloomsbury. These latter promises were always fanciful but necessary parts of the public proposition. Flimsy as they later proved to be, the overall grandeur of the scheme was rewarded with a £30 million Millennium grant in July. By October, Claus Moser could tell trustees that £106 million of the £108 million fundraising target had been reached. This was by any standards of fundraising an extraordinary achievement reflecting Moser's skills but also pointed to a huge reservoir of support for the very idea of the British Museum.

But a new controversy erupted that threatened to tarnish the hoped-for glory of the Great Court. In June 1999, Chris Jones, Head of Administration, warned trustees that a significant element of the Great Court, the entirely new internal entrance known as the 'South Portico', was not built of Portland Stone as contracted but a stone very close to it, similar perhaps, but the colour was noticeably different. The public story became simply that the BM had got 'the wrong stone'. It was a public relations disaster, yet another example, it was charged by some in the press, of the Museum's general incompetence. The trustees had to sort this one out by themselves: it was their crisis, it must be their solution. The DCMS had no standing in the matter so relations in Whitehall were not at issue yet again. This was something of a relief. Corporate and private funders were not going to help out.

The issue was in one sense simple and in every other sense complex: the stone for the South Portico was definitely not Portland. It might be similar geologically, another 'oolitic limestone', but it was not Portland. On the other hand, it did come from the Portland seam after it emerged on the other side of the Channel in France. Interesting, but academic. Whatever its source, it undoubtedly looked more yellowish than the rest of the Great Court. Some sort of common position had to be reached.

Camden Council, the planning authority with whom the Museum had a strikingly poor relationship, wanted the portico pulled down. Chris Jones warned the trustees that it would cost £3 million to do so and would trigger countless claims from other contractors for enforced delays. The internal debate was intense and ran over many months. John Boyd felt the stone contractor should be sued. Keith Thomas believed it was the architect's responsibility to ensure it was the right stone, while

Martin Rees was of the view that if the argument was about aesthetics, it didn't matter; if it was about reputation for competence, then it did. Michael Hopkins, the architect trustee, felt the stone looked good. The architect directly responsible, Spencer de Grey, argued that since the South Portico was an entirely new element in the Great Court that fact should be acknowledged – the 'wrong stone', if that was what it was, honestly proclaimed the fact that it was new. (This was an argument less fashionable then than it is today.)

The dispute turned on one opinion, one fact. The common-sense opinion came from the artist, Tom Phillips. He could never understand why he was put on the Great Court Committee in the first place when all the key decisions had already been taken. As he and John Browne stood in the middle of the Great Court, Browne looked at the existing walls of weathered, dappled stone and asked, 'How can you get an exact match?' Phillips replied: 'You can't, because the weathering and mottling of existing stone have come from years of ageing in the open air.' From now on, the Great Court would be enclosed by its glass roof. There would be no weathering, no possibility of any new stone matching the old, wherever it came from.

The immovable fact was that HM The Queen was set to open the Great Court in December 2000. Chairman Graham Greene made that very clear: nothing would put the royal opening at risk. The reputational cost would be massive, the project had to come in on time. Claus Moser and his development team led by Director of Corporate Affairs Sukie Hemming declared the £108 million fundraising target to have been reached. The rising costs were another matter. As Chair of the Audit Committee, John Browne interviewed architect Norman Foster about the 'cost estimates starting to go through the ceiling'. Foster replied, according to Browne, that there were always risks to the estimates on such a complex building and that the board had not listened to them.

Armed with this warning, Browne then led discussions about how to reduce rising costs, how to control them and how to estimate future costs accurately. He concluded the project had always been seriously and riskily under-managed on the Museum side. Given its notorious managerial shortcomings, he turned to one of the principal funders, Garfield Weston, for support. Weston asked for assurance that a proper project manager would bring the project in 'on target'. Browne duly installed a BP project manager as part of his company's corporate support and the Great Court costs were brought under control in a close call that reflected poorly on existing BM governance and management. However, the claim that the project was 'on cost' was tenuous; digging deep into the numbers, the accountant David Lindsell discovered that several millions of the Great Court costs were hidden under budget lines for 'other expenditure'. At least it was certainly 'on time'. Greene's insistence on sticking to the original schedule was from this point of view vindicated.

The Royal Opening by HM The Queen on 6 December 2000 was a glittering affair. The roof, with each glass panel appearing identical but actually each different in proportion, was rightly greeted as a 'technological wonder'; the newly stone-encased Reading Room flanked by sweeping staircases bathed in a brilliant light; the surrounding spaces were generous, warm and romantic rather than intimidating. Harmoniously proportioned, it was elegantly balanced, grand but welcoming. It appeared as if this had been intended to look like this since the beginning. The previously hostile press could only wonder and approve. Visitors poured in. None observed then or since that the South Portico stone was the 'wrong' colour.

But success had been achieved despite the British Museum's governance structures rather than as a vindication of them. The trustees could claim little credit for delivering the Great Court; it was not even the achievement of a properly constituted sub-committee. It is generally agreed by all those involved that a group of just three people – chairman Graham Greene, fundraiser-in-chief Claus Moser and the architect, Norman Foster, delivered a project that would shape the Museum for decades to come. Trustees were kept informed but otherwise left out of any decision-making loop. Some would argue that the Greene/Moser/ Foster group deserve only thanks and admiration for doing what neither management nor governance structure in their existing forms could have done. According to John Browne: 'Claus and Graham absolutely ran it together.' Keith Thomas agrees and adds: 'Most of the business was not conducted at the Board but "offstage" by Graham and Claus. We didn't complain loudly enough.' David Norgrove recalls, 'The Trustees didn't control the development of Great Court as they should have done.' Other trustees, including the artist Tom Phillips, endorsed that judgement.

My own recollection is of the key influence of the third member of the 'group of three', the architect, Norman Foster. Moser often said to me: 'Norman is a great architect and if Norman wants it, it should be done.' Few would dispute the first part of that sentiment but allowing an architect to play such a dominant role in a project, above even the direct needs of the client, goes against all norms and practice. Suzanna Taverne insists that Foster knew that his real client was Claus Moser rather than the Museum: 'Since Moser and Greene wanted glory for the Museum, they were not very interested in making the budget work' – or in some of the dreary practical needs of the Museum. When Price Waterhouse Cooper (PWC) reviewed the Great Court scheme late in 2000, they observed that the Greene/Moser Working Committee had acted in an 'executive capacity'. Since this was at best a sub-committee of the main board, it should have had no executive role. Moser denied it had, but most recognized the PWC comment as valid; he might have responded in the manner of the architect

Sir Christopher Wren when looking around St Paul's: 'If you want a justification, look around you!'

At its next major project, five years later, the £125 million World Conservation and Exhibition Centre, the British Museum was to run things in a wholly different way. Lessons had been learned from the Great Court project, brilliant as it was. This time the project had to have truly professional oversight and be properly connected to the board. Above all, the architect must become the servant of the client.

Dazzling as the new Great Court was, the way that it was managed had serious and practical consequences. With his background in retail from Marks & Spencer, David Norgrove was shocked to find that in planning the Great Court, 'the retail was an afterthought'. Taverne adds that other shortcomings in the scheme included facilities for catering, visitor circulation and signage. All these matters should have been high on the list of client needs, but seem not to have been deemed a priority for Moser or Greene. If the client did not speak up for them, why should the architect design them? Yet in Norgrove's experience, there needed to be no tension between practical needs and architectural vision: 'The things that are wrong with Great Court might not have been difficult to fix if they had been done at the time of construction.' Nor, he added, did it need to weaken the dynamics of the fundraising: 'You could have raised the money without compromising on the needs of the museum provided you defined more clearly what those needs were.'

Brilliant as the construction of the Great Court was, the trustees still had three further major tasks facing them in 2001: to bring the budget deficit under control, to accept that governance had to be reformed and to change the leadership, ending the disastrous separation of powers between nominal director and actual managing director.

In a sense the first was the easiest: trustees could no longer ignore the looming multi-million annual deficit nor pretend that it could be eliminated without shedding staff on a large scale. Those days were over. At the start of 2002, the capable Head of Administration and later Accounting Officer, Chris Jones, advised that with a deficit of £5 million, or 11 per cent of the annual expenditure, that deficit was structural, not temporary. Putting it right would involve savings of 15 per cent from every department and 30 per cent from some. Jones warned against dodging the reality by hoping that income generation might close some of the gap, the customary delusional avoidance mechanism. Trustees agreed there would be 'no "no-go" areas when looking for savings'. This was a mighty change of attitude from their approach a few years back. Reality was breaking in due in large part to Jones' quiet authority.

By April 2002, Jones had refined his proposals: £3.55 million of the savings were classified as Category 1, that is to say essential; a further £2.45 million might be classified as Category 2, but come what may, a total of £6 million had to be delivered. The trustees' only reservation was to urge that 'curatorial skills and staff should be protected'. His blueprint for reform delivered, Chris Jones stepped aside. His successors were to implement it, but he had set the direction. It was a considerable achievement of quiet, thorough, professional management – the Museum owed him a great deal.

It was time to make the BM's governance work in a way that was true to its past but suited to the complexities of the museum world of the new millennium. No one was going to repeal the British Museum Act of 1753; the number of trustees would stay at 25; the rules and conventions for appointing them would not change. What could be done to improve matters? John Browne, who was asked to draw up proposals for change, reflected: 'If we have the board as we do, it should meet infrequently. Somehow, they had to delegate authority to a smaller group of people who could get things done and really sit on top of what was going on.' His final model proposed just four meetings a year for the full board, a standing committee with full powers and strong committees for audit, nominations and governance.

To the objection that Browne was diminishing the role of trustees, he replied: 'The principle thing was to get a smaller decision-making time frame, getting the Trustees out of departments. This would allow them to advise as board members. I had this line that the Board has no authority until it sits together. When it does, it has authority. I had to bend over backwards to get these people, mainly academics to get out of the day-to-day, which they liked. They didn't like the bigger picture.'

Two organizational blueprints were thus in place by mid-2002: for bringing the budget under control and for modernizing the way the board could exercise its supervisory functions. These were big steps. Who would put them into practice? Before answering that question, the final moments of the compromise duumvirate flared into psycho-drama. They involved the standing and future of the managing director, Suzanna Taverne. Her contract was a permanent one, but she recognized that on Anderson's departure the dual structure would not remain.

Taverne was immensely proud of the part she had played in delivering the Great Court, but, in her words, the trustees 'never even had the guts to say to me that these are the reasons we have decided to change the structure, these are the qualities we need and these are the reasons why we are approaching somebody else.' Invited – rather belatedly, she feels – to apply for a directorship which she felt was already destined for Neil MacGregor, Taverne resigned at the end of 2001.

I recall that knowledge of Suzanna's open ambition to become director was well known, strongly resented and did not help her cause. Her own conclusion remains that the trustees' failure to support her in any way lacked 'basic human or professional decency'. In this, Taverne feels she experienced the 'phenomenon known as the "glass cliff", the advanced version of the glass ceiling'. Defined simply, 'if you have a real challenge, which is frankly designed for failure, then it is quite a clever thing to find a half-way competent woman to take it on.' At the end when rejection looms the response is 'You didn't think, did you, that you were going to continue to do this job? How silly, but you are only a slip of a girl'.

Taverne left the Museum on 31 December 2001. The best that can be said about the way the Anderson/Taverne duumvirate ended was that it was necessary but the British Museum's handling of it was uncaring, undignified and unprofessional.

By 2002, it felt as if a new era was becoming possible. Chairman Graham Greene and Director Robert Anderson retired. Each left with the trustees' plaudits in their ears. Greene was praised for 'great perspicacity and commitment throughout his chairmanship', Anderson for his 'fantastic achievement of Great Court and maintaining the Museum's scholarly standards and values'. He probably received less credit than he deserved for also initiating the restoration of the King's Library project in the Museum's east wing. It would be for entirely new leadership to implement the programme of budgetary reductions and to modernize governance. They would now have solid foundations to build on.

The hope had been for John Browne, the most heavyweight of business executives and architect of the BM's governance reform, to succeed Greene as chairman. This fell through when word came that the BP Board thought this unacceptable for the company, one of the largest in the world. Browne insists that he himself took the decision because he 'had a real job to do. I assessed what the [BP] Board would say without asking them. It would have been out of the question. I was the CEO of BP. To take on the chairmanship of the BM, every investor in the world would have said, "What on earth is going on here?"' Some Trustees though had the impression that he was a real candidate with a strong personal interest in the position.

The chairmanship position went to Sir John Boyd, trustee, a distinguished former ambassador in Tokyo and Master of Churchill College, Cambridge. Highly persuasive, scholarly and in every sense diplomatic as he was, Boyd seemed well-suited to the complex tasks of reconciling differences within such a diverse institution as the British Museum. He also had unparalleled connections with Japan, China and South Korea from his diplomatic career. But he had suffered a serious stroke in November 2000. Was he fit to take on a major non-executive role as well as heading a big Cambridge college?

His wife, Julia Boyd, says she had 'considerable reservations' about his becoming chairman. But the appointment 'did more for his recovery than any medicine or physio' and apart from a limp and a stick, Boyd was 'fully functioning' as Master of Churchill College before he took over at the BM. In fact, she insists the effects of the stroke were always physical not mental: 'He started learning Korean two days after the stroke happened.' There was never, in my experience, the slightest sign of mental slowness in Boyd's chairing of the BM trustees. Helena Kennedy praises his charm and ability to pick up the pieces of a tricky situation. He was, she believes, moved by an old-fashioned sense of duty to do his best by a great public institution. For his part, Boyd conceded the demands of the job involving frequent train journeys from Cambridge were stressful. He would never recommend a position that involved so much train travel.

The first task was to find a director who would once more have full authority to lead the Museum. Boyd recalled, 'We had become a laughing stock, the object of press scorn.' The hiring process was very thorough – it had to be. At the final interviews, we saw three strong candidates, all with real track records in museums or galleries. Boyd had taken the precaution of consulting staff before appointing. They all wanted a 'strong director'. In choosing Neil MacGregor from the National Gallery, we knew we had found one.

In some aspects, the Boyd/MacGregor team was less than perfectly matched, the radicalism and energy of the director matched poorly with the practised caution of the diplomat chairman. One trustee at least knew what to expect. The Oxford historian, Keith Thomas, had sat on the board of the National Gallery and observed MacGregor and his relationship with that gallery's chairman, Jacob Rothschild. According to Thomas, 'Rothschild was a very strong chairman. Neil was wonderful at talking to National Gallery supporters but he had less freedom of action. He was the servant of the board more than he would be at the BM. But he was not keen on trustees as an institution.' But if directing the National Gallery under strong guidance was the loftiest kind of apprenticeship in the gallery world, Thomas adds drily, 'Neil had learned the nuances of Board/Director relationships rather better.' He knew how to manage them too.

Certainly, his new chairman was no Jacob Rothschild and John Boyd felt the sheer force of personality of his new director very early on: 'He wanted to run the Museum. Right from the start, he wanted to keep the Board at a respectful distance. That changed over time.' Recently, John Boyd observed 'It was not always easy' though others look back fondly to the '"John and Neil" time'. For his part, MacGregor viewed their relationship with realism and without sentimentality: 'John Boyd was an admirable man but one who had another full-time job, which involved fundraising in exactly comparable areas and a man who had a severe stroke, limited energy and limited time. It was a very strange choice by the Trustees to choose this chairman at a critical moment.'

Perhaps the explanation is simpler than it seems. Once Browne became unavailable, the trustees felt they had to appoint a chairman whose urgent first task would be to appoint a director. That certainly could not wait. In the circumstances, quite apart from John Boyd's considerable merits, the trustees surely got their priorities right.

One further appointment was needed: a deputy director who would run the Museum in all the ways that the Edwards report had found wanting. Dawn Austwick had recently completed the task of project managing the creation of Tate Modern from an abandoned power station. It was a huge achievement. She needed no further credentials. When approached about the position, Austwick was wary because of the Museum's image: 'For me, the BM seemed like this sort of institution that existed across time and we all went to as children. Actually, it didn't really have a relationship with society and that was what interested me about culture.' But once MacGregor had 'conjured his wand and created this extraordinary vision for what the Museum could be', reservations vanished and she was hooked.

Specifically, Austwick's task was to implement the agreed deficit reduction programme to save £6 million. It had to be completed in two years and it was. Lightly and misleadingly, she described her role as deputy to MacGregor as 'sorting out a lot of the gubbins'. However, it is impossible to overstate her importance in the BM's leadership, in the Museum's recovery or her value to the director. It freed him to do what he did best: 'conjure a wand and create a vision'.

Before he did that, MacGregor took one prudent step. He was determined to mend the British Museum's drastically poor relations with the DCMS – they were, after all, joint accounting officers for the BM in Whitehall. Dawn Austwick, he recalls, played a crucial role in persuading the department that the BM would be managed efficiently and rigorously: 'She put her own credit on the line with the DCMS.' MacGregor added: 'They had no confidence in how the place was run and they were right to have no confidence. I wouldn't sort the BM out in two years, but within those two years it would not be helpful to have an external review going on from the DCMS.' They agreed. He also asked to be consulted about government appointments to the board 'as it was clear we needed a different board'. And for good measure, he asked for consultation about the chairman after John Boyd.

With his political back secured, MacGregor could start painting the vision. Some boards believe that defining the 'mission' is their responsibility and role. I have never believed this; Neil certainly did not either. From his very first board meeting 'in attendance' in February 2002, he declared his belief that 'the 1753 Enlightenment Dream remained proclaimable and truer today than in the last 250 years'. At subsequent meetings, he called on the Louvre and the National Museums in Berlin to join the BM in making the case for 'universal museums'. The need for universality to make the world's cultural patrimony available to all was more urgent than ever. He also positioned the BM as the 'mother of world museums' emphasizing that the Museum's role in international relations could not be overstated: 'If properly funded, it could provide important political benefits for the United Kingdom.'

In laying the ground of his vision so early, so clearly and so ambitiously in his directorship, Neil MacGregor was doing at least three things. First, the notion of universality challenged the widespread belief held by museums elsewhere that they were principally expressions of national culture and identity. Universality was a different proposition placed in the frontline of defence against claims for restitution of objects often based on nationalism. Second, rooting the British Museum in its historical origins of the Enlightenment and its legal foundation by Act of Parliament reminded all of its duty to resist day-to-day modish political pressures. Third, by identifying the BM's potential role in international relations, he opened the door to an exhibition policy as culturally daring as it proved politically effective. There was also a fourth and more local purpose: to reassure trustees that the Museum under its new director had a regained sense of purpose and direction.

Today, MacGregor declines the customarily applied label of 'cultural diplomacy' to describe what he did: 'It suggests that we operate on the French model of cultural institutions being instruments of the state. That is why they exist.' By contrast, the British Museum model, he insists, 'is an affirmation of the republic of letters. It was an attempt to demonstrate again and again that there is a republic of letters which is quite separate from the political realm.' More prosaically, according to Keith Thomas, 'Neil was very good at saying "this [exhibition] can help with British diplomacy" and the FCO loved it.'

No one should underestimate the political value and importance of laying the ground for your actions in theory and in law. MacGregor was not trained as a lawyer for nothing. He also knew that more immediate and urgent signals about the British Museum's purposes needed making.

The BM's letterhead had as its strapline 'Illuminating World Cultures'. I always thought it dreary and banal beyond belief, the product surely of a very unimaginative consultancy. For me, it could not be replaced too soon but there was no indication that it would be. One day, so it seemed at the time, a new strapline emerged fully formed from Neil MacGregor's mouth. What was the British Museum? Why 'A Museum of the World for the World'. Universality, inclusiveness, generosity, all in one phrase. Legitimacy too. Did not the 1753 Act speak of a museum for 'all studious and curious persons, native and foreign'? There it was, there it had been from the very beginning. I recall no discussion with the trustees on the subject of a new strapline. Today, MacGregor insists that it came as a result of internal discussion with colleagues. At the time the trustees were more than happy to greet it as another sign of their director's brilliance. We needed a vision, here it was. David Norgrove reflects the view of most: 'Neil transformed the reputation of the Museum not just by flim-flam, but by giving it a sense of purpose, a better sense of what it was for.'

By mid-decade of the new millennium, the trustees could feel that three parts of the renewal programme were in place though it was never known as that. A new director was establishing his authority, defining a vision, mending relations with Whitehall and earning golden opinions from the media. A new deputy director was running the administration, implementing savings and balancing the budget. Trustees were in place on key board committees and exercising their proper supervisory role. One further element was needed: a new chairman to succeed John Boyd.

The reality was that he and MacGregor were never ideally suited. Boyd's somewhat reserved comments later reflected that fact: 'Love him or not, Neil is a genius in his way. I had to work hard on the relationship.' As a close-up witness of the Boyd/MacGregor relationship, Dawn Austwick concluded: 'The partnership wasn't catastrophic and the Museum moved forward. These things are about chemistry and relationships and my observation would be that they didn't bring out the best in each other and that limited John's ability to flourish.' John Browne's conclusion is that Boyd presided over a very important transition in the BM's affairs: 'He did a good job, he understood what he was doing and was a consummate diplomat.' Tom Phillips recalls him as a 'good listener', preferable to the 'clubby world' embodied by his predecessor, Graham Greene. My own view is that Boyd's sense of public duty made calls on him of a demanding kind. His conduct was admirable beyond words. He was just not the right chairman for Neil MacGregor. Could the trustees find one who would be?

When headhunters approached Niall FitzGerald to talk about his becoming chairman of the British Museum, they were stalking the biggest of big business game. Not content with having been Chairman and CEO of Unilever, one of the world's largest companies, he was now Chairman of Reuters. If caught for the BM, FitzGerald would be a very big catch indeed.

At first he was cautious, concerned at his lack of knowledge of what the Museum was in practice. FitzGerald identified three questions for himself: 'Is it intellectually interesting? Can I make a specific contribution which comes from my background or experience? Finally, is it fun, something that would engage me?' Each question had to have a positive tick for him to proceed.

There was something else, the most important question of all. Was the chemistry between him and Neil MacGregor good; did they share the same values and vision? From long business experience, he knew that 'unless shared values exist between Chair and CEO, the organization doesn't function'. To considerable amazement within the Museum, FitzGerald spent 'several months' on his reconnaissance. This involved a 'long series of "get togethers" with Neil over several weeks' to make sure they were complementary in outlook and skills and wouldn't get in one another's way. He began to conclude that 'I was very different, came from outside, had a very different skillset which was needed by the museum. It still allowed Neil to do what he was so extraordinarily good at doing and I think that is what made it work.'

On his side, MacGregor was struck by FitzGerald's 'prodigious experience based on working with people'. If the British Museum was about scholarship and objects it was also about people. More importantly, 'Niall is a very open man and a man who is very humble in the face of the institution. He had absolutely no vanity in the face of the BM, he knew this was much bigger than he was.'

On the night before FitzGerald was to make his decision, he and MacGregor dined together. He had one final question for the director: 'If I say "yes", will you be there for at least five years because this is very important to me in terms of how we will work together?' MacGregor's response, as FitzGerald recalls it: 'In a very Neil-like way he said, "the answer is yes if you say yes", which was a moment of contracting between us.' Liz Forgan concluded: 'The real thing about the Niall/Neil era was that they worked really hard on the nature of their relationship, they had done all their talking through and thinking through before Niall took the job.'

What did they find in one another? Liz Forgan's judgement on the two people, first the chairman? 'Niall was very smart, very self-confident, very charming, passionate about the organization, humble in the face of academic brilliance, courageous himself and fostering a board where all were encouraged to speak and be frank.' And Forgan's measured verdict on the director: 'Neil had a completely brilliant vision for the institution. Academic qualifications not of the very first order but hugely respected everywhere. Oratorical eloquence and a brilliant ability to articulate the purpose of the museum.' Her conclusion was that the FitzGerald/MacGregor team was 'as near a perfect partnership of these two functions as I have ever seen'. The lesson is that it did not happen by luck or accident. It had been the result of time, hard work, deep thought, soul-searching and personal honesty.

It had been a long, painful 10 years from the Edwards report's damaging revelations of British Museum management and governance failings in 1996 to the establishment of the FitzGerald/MacGregor leadership in 2006. At the end, John Browne thought a necessary clarity had been achieved: 'The chair manages the board, the executive manages the management.' As FitzGerald put it: 'I absolutely accepted that the vision of the Museum was Neil's; I could help in finance, I could help build the enabling things we needed to do to reach that vision. But it was Neil's.' He could also help in building competence in the Museum's management team, both for immediate and future needs.

Two strong people met. Some feared they might clash. Both were 'pretty pushy,' observed one trustee. Rather than fighting, they complemented each other's skills. MacGregor could acknowledge his own needs: 'Every director is going to feel lonely. You need a chairman who can see where the director is struggling and can help him.'

Having established this clarity of function, FitzGerald could then complete the reform of governance set out by John Browne. The full board would meet just four times a year. In between times, a standing committee of three vice chairmen, of whom I was one, and three trustees on rotation, conducted regular business. The specialist committees continued as recommended by Browne. Further clarity was provided by identifying those matters reserved to the board, those reserved to the standing committee and those delegated to the executive.

What this meant for the director was that the board could invite distinguished international trustees who might expect to attend four meetings a year but not more, people such as Amartya Sen, the Indian economist, and Chief Emeka Anyoku from Nigeria, the former Commonwealth Secretary-General. Such appointments, for MacGregor, were 'of enormous value as well as enormous symbolic importance' for a museum 'of the world and for the world'.

It also meant that individual trustees could be used to make significant contributions. With Greek demands for the return of the Parthenon Sculptures a constant issue, FitzGerald received an invitation from the new Hellenic Museum in Athens to attend its celebratory opening in December 2011. It was obvious that his presence would become the focus of a public dispute about restitution of the sculptures. Finding a plausible reason not to attend himself, FitzGerald asked if the Museum could send a deputy chair in his place: 'Imagine the Greeks' consternation when a small, black, female writer from the south side of Chicago arrived, Bonnie Greer! There wasn't a great deal the Greeks could say that this was the representative of an imperial institution. Bonnie did a brilliant job.'

I recall another decisive intervention from a particular trustee. The Blair government regularly urged the Museum to compromise by offering

Greece a loan of the Parthenon sculptures. During a general discussion about the possibility of a temporary loan, the Greek-Cypriot archaeologist Edmée Leventis spoke up in these words: 'Please let me advise you. Even if the Greek Government absolutely committed itself legally to returning a loan of the sculptures, once they were in Greece, return would be impossible. Any government would fall if it tried to return them.' It was a key contribution to the discussion.

This instance confirmed Liz Forgan's observation which pointed to an important central paradox of governance: 'The big board was fantastically useful because each individual member could be asked to do things that only they could do. The board could move mountains, individually.'

By the time I left the board in 2009, I could look back on a near-decade of turmoil, transition and finally, transformation. The British Museum now had a chairman and director who collaborated and filled in the other's weaknesses, strong and effective management and trustees who supervised, but did not interfere. As a result, the BM's reputation shed its earlier pall of gloom and took a place in the topmost ranks among its peers worldwide. If the trustees had been slow to come to terms with the demands of modern museum management, they had adapted even if they did so only just in time. Should change have happened more quickly? Probably. But perhaps no more could be asked of a 250-year-old body. As Martin Rees observed, 'All these structures are rather fragile.'

And yet one human quality was found to be wanting – generosity. On Neil MacGregor's departure as director in 2015, media coverage was rightly highly laudatory. Some of the comment seemed to go out of its way to belittle or disparage the BM's previous leadership. This annoyed Robert Anderson, the former director and at least two trustees, Keith Thomas and Martin Rees. After all, who had built the Great Court and much else besides? In a letter to Anderson, Rees recalled 'being furious that at the dinner for the fifth anniversary of the Great Court, none of the four speakers mentioned you, Graham or Claus'. John Boyd deeply regrets that he accepted the advice he was given by Museum officials not to refer to the previous regime in his speech, but he did include a sentence saying 'the scheme stood on the shoulders of giants'.

With this slight still fresh in some memories, when MacGregor was receiving all the praise for the BM's success, Keith Thomas wrote to *The Times* in April 2015, reminding readers of the practical achievements of the Greene/Anderson years, adding, 'Neil MacGregor brought unique qualities to the Directorship but his brilliant success would not have been possible without these earlier developments.' Martin Rees wrote in similar vein and says he received an apologetic letter from MacGregor. Rees concludes, 'Distortion was unfair to his predecessor.' There is no evidence that the laudatory media coverage came from a deliberate steer from the Museum itself. It makes a sad if tiny footnote to a brilliant period in the BM's history. Sometimes it is difficult for a new leadership to acknowledge their predecessors' achievements.

Management could now move on, in Dawn Austwick's words, 'to embed the vision deep into the curatorial stages of the organization, and to move from cost-cutting to income generating.'

The value of the trustee system was validated for Neil MacGregor, incomparably the best model: 'The greatest benefit is in having a group of people who can challenge the executive to fulfil the purposes of the place and defend and advance those purposes against the outside world.' Governance itself could also now move on, in David Norgrove's view, from its prevalent 'stop-the-disasters' mode to taking the organization forward: 'That's not just about governance, that's about the character of the people you appoint and above all, the character of the Chair.'

A final perspective is required if the actions and behaviour of the British Museum's leadership are to be fairly assessed. The widespread assumption is that museums are merely rather large arts organizations, that they are not difficult to run and running a business is far harder. Few are better placed to challenge this view than the former CEO of British Petroleum, John Browne, and the former Marks & Spencer director, David Norgrove.

Given that the BM's turnover was of the order of £50 million a year, running it, according to Browne, was 'twenty times more complex than running a £50 million business'. He explained this interesting assertion by setting out five layers of complexity in the running of a museum: first, the purely commercial, exhibition ticket sales, shops, catering; second, a museum was not an entertainment place only, it was an enlightened place that built on academic expertise; third, it had to create access, make things accessible for the public. The fourth level involved acting in line with an ever-changing government view of what the cultural sector was meant to contribute to society. Finally, a museum had to keep all its stakeholders aligned because if it raised money from someone that suddenly became controversial, crisis would occur.

For David Norgrove, the Museum's objectives are certainly more complex than a business but also inherently more in conflict with each other: 'The BM has to preserve objects and to show them (one conflict); hold exhibitions that advance scholarship and don't lose too much money (another); keep Government on side but maintain independence (yet another); all within public sector accountability constraints and a lack of money that would startle any reasonably successful business.' Clearly, another potential ground of conflict.

If people from the world of business, such as Browne and Norgrove, identify the difficulties in these ways, who can ever again say that running a museum is simpler or easier than running a company?

All these layers of complexity and potential areas of conflict had to be overseen by what was by its nature, in Martin Rees' observation, a 'fragile body'. The wonder is not that there were stumbles along the road of recovery but the 10-year transformation of the BM's vision, finances, systems, leadership, governance and fortunes took place as it did. Once the trustees had put their house in order, perhaps the British Museum once more had the right to be regarded as 'too grand to fail'.

REFLECTIONS

Governance must keep up with the times. Make changes before events force you to do so.

Few governance systems last very long. Assume they will need reviewing every decade.

Trustees should ask who are the true beneficiaries of the institution. The answer will shape how it acts.

Trustees should know why they have been invited to join the board and how they might best contribute. One contribution on a single issue may be decisive.

Just because other trustees are distinguished doesn't mean you have no role to play.

Be clear with yourself and the institution about the time you can commit to trusteeship. Shape your contribution in relation to the time you do have available.

Trustees should not assume the institution is more important than it is or that it is beyond criticism.

Do not assume funders will support them without good cause and have no right to know what they are up to.

No institution, however venerable, is too grand to be allowed to fail.

When the time comes to appoint a new chairman or director, consider whether new terms of reference for each position should be drawn up. Does an opportunity exist for a change of direction?

Take time over appointing a chairman or director. Lots of time. Don't appoint unless you know you have the right person.

Trustees should defend their institution's independence. Government pressure should be resisted. If you do pick a quarrel with the government, make sure of the ground you stand on.

Ensure chairman and director are compatible. Make one-to-one discussions between future chairman and director part of the appointment process. If chairman and director are incompatible, think hard about starting again.

No chairman should think they are better or bigger than the organization they head.

Chairmen need to give their time to the organization in order to understand it, but never to think that they are running it.

No director will have all the skills needed to do the job. Make sure the necessary management skills exist elsewhere in the organization to support the director.

In a major capital scheme, responsibility cannot be subcontracted from the main board to a small group, however brilliant. In a major capital project, the architect is the servant of the client and is there to meet the client's needs.

If the client does not know their needs or fails to set them out, no architect can be expected to meet them. Without direction from the client, the architect will set their own.

If a mission statement sounds dull, get a new one.

Every institution exists in a continuum of activity. Be generous to those who ran the place before you – they may have laid the basis for things you did.

The main board has full authority. That does not mean it should interfere in how the organization works, though.

Trustees should get to know the staff; they will be better trustees as a result. But the museum as a whole always comes first.

Taking part in an organization with effective governance is less stressful and more satisfying than in one without.

Trustees will make mistakes. This matters less than their ability to learn from them.

Museums are more complex than businesses of a similar size. They face layers of accountability, which often threaten to conflict with one another.

5

The Wigmore Years: Chairmanship is Harder Than You Think (1999–2011)

Interviews with

Aubrey Adams, Trustee, Chairman (2011–present); Chief Executive, Savills plc.

Tony Allen, Accountant, Price Waterhouse Coopers; Development Committee 1994, Trustee 1999–present

Paula Best, House Manager, Head of Publications and Archive, 1985–2018

Lady Hilary Browne-Wilkinson, lawyer, Trustee

John Gilhooly, Director, 2005–present

David King, Senior House Manager, 1985–2019

Marie-Helene Osterweil, Head of Development, 2001, Director of Development 2005–present

Cita Stelzer, Trustee

By the late 1990s, I was settled into my role as managing director of the Barbican Centre, my second position as a chief executive following the

BBC World Service. During that time, I had experienced a variety of forms of governance and had observed and endured service under many chairs of major arts organizations. It had been a varied, occasionally bewildering experience.

There was no single model, no assured formula for success, no guarantee of satisfaction, personal or professional. For years, I had observed, commented, criticized, lamented, warned and perhaps learned from the relatively carefree security of 'mere' board membership. I was about to be invited to take up a chairman's role, to move from observation to responsibility. As Chair of the Trustees of the Wigmore Hall from 1999, I would be tested to the full and would fail several of those tests.

There were many reasons to accept the invitation to chair the Wigmore Hall. It presented music that my wife, Ann, and I loved, it presented artistes we admired, and it discovered and nurtured the performers of coming generations. It would be a pleasure and a privilege to try and help the Hall to flourish. A hall of 550 seats with a chamber music, piano and song remit could not have been further in nature from the Barbican, with its 2,000-seat concert hall, symphony orchestra, world music and theatre repertoire. It represented no conflict of interest for me, no competition for audiences, no fighting for sponsors. Wigmore Hall was part-funded by Westminster City Council; the Barbican mainly by the City of London. If ever there was a natural fit, it was surely for me to manage the Barbican and chair Wigmore side by side. Most importantly, Wigmore's history would show that while governance good or bad throws up its own difficulties, the absence of it guarantees frustration and stagnation.

Different as they were, the two venues had one aspect in common. They were both young in governance terms: the Barbican just 13 years old as a place and organization; Wigmore just six years old as an independent charity with its own board. There, the similarities ran out. Although the

Hall was almost a century old, opening in 1901, its existence through the decades had been fraught. Buffeted by events which sometimes challenged its very existence, it lacked a supervisory board to assist in the fight for survival.

Founded as the Bechstein Hall in 1901 by the German piano company of the same name, it was impounded and closed by the Official Receiver at the outbreak of the First World War in 1914. In 1916, the neighbouring department store Debenham's bought it for less than it cost to build and prudently renamed it Wigmore Hall after the London street in which it stood. For a decade or more it housed variety and novelty performances with large quantities of 'paper' filling many of the seats. So-called 'serious concerts' were dismissed as a 'ragbag' by the press, the place described as oozing 'gentility and cultivated amateurishness'. Its audiences were dismissed as having 'limited aspirations or powers of concentration'.

By the 1950s, lacking any standing, reputation or real artistic purpose, it was suggested that Wigmore Hall might be used for annual general meetings. Why any company should have wanted to hire a hall known mainly for its 'worn-out carpets and old central heating' was never explained. By the 1970s, *The Times* dismissed the Hall as being known only for its 'spate of inopportune debut' concerts. A nadir of sorts was surely reached in 1973 when *Melody Maker* noted the 'Wigmore Hall was an unusual place, more like a luxurious funeral parlour than a concert auditorium'. The mystery is that the Hall survived at all for three-quarters of a century with such a dismal record of non-achievement.

That it did survive was due to one incontestable fact and one extraordinary person. The fact was that the Hall was an acoustic masterpiece. Designed by the architect Thomas Collcutt, the promotional material described it as 'the most commodious and from an acoustic point of view the most perfect concert hall in London'. Unusually, the press agreed, judging the Wigmore to be 'the handsomest concert room'. Collcutt had designed a simple 'shoe box', slightly longer than it is wide, then and now the classic shape for good acoustics. For more than a century, performers and listeners alike have judged Wigmore's acoustics to be beyond criticism. But acoustic excellence was insufficient in itself. Major international performers did occasionally appear, but the Hall lacked an overall purpose, any coherent artistic programming, any budget or any formal governance.

The extraordinary person was a young Australian, William Lyne. Trained for a decade by the long-time hall manager H.T.C. Brickell, the post became vacant in 1966. Lyne impressed the Arts Council at his interview – they had never shown any interest in or commitment to the Hall as an arts organization – and was duly appointed. They could not have known what they were doing. As the great artists' manager, Robert Rattray, wrote later, instead of appointing 'an Arts Council apparatchik with minimal experience and less knowledge', they lighted on 'a very special young man, unique, professional, mild of manner, exceptional vision, resolute and unwavering determination'.

Lyne would need all of these qualities in the often-lonely years ahead. He introduced a monthly concert diary – previously unknown – centralized ticket sales and started Sunday evening concerts. The Arts Council gave him no funding for artists' fees – save the opening concert of the season from 1975 – and offered no supervisory support in the form of governance. They checked the financial numbers and carried out Human Relations (HR) functions – that was the extent of their involvement. If there is one thing worse than bad governance, it is the absence of governance. That is one of the lessons of Wigmore Hall's long, desolate years when being a concert hall without any structure to guide and direct it proved so sterile.

The Arts Council's lack of commitment to Wigmore Hall's artistic potential revealed itself a year after Lyne's appointment as manager. The imposing new Queen Elizabeth Hall opened in all its concrete severity on the South Bank in March 1967. With its additional small recital venue, the Purcell Room, the *Observer* stated bluntly: 'The QEH sounds the death knell for the Wigmore Hall.' If that was to be its fate, nobody in the music world cared, certainly not the Arts Council. Nobody spoke up for the best acoustics in London, far better than anything ever achieved on the South Bank. Reading the *Observer*'s dismissal of Wigmore's future, prediction of its imminent demise, William Lyne declared: 'I'll see if it does! Competition goaded me to strive even harder.'

Perhaps one of Lyne's most daring acts was on the occasion of the Hall's 75th anniversary in 1976. Almost alone in believing it worthy of celebration, Lyne simply wrote to the great Polish-American virtuoso pianist, Artur Rubinstein, at the very height of his reputation, inviting him to give the anniversary recital. It was a sign of the Hall's extraordinary submerged reputation that Rubinstein agreed to perform, 'without fee or expenses'. If this jolted the Arts Council into recognition of the Wigmore's potential, they did nothing to support it.

A decade later, the Arts Council finally washed its hands of the Hall and handed it over to Westminster City Council. The detailed transfer document in August 1987 specified that Westminster City Council would 'undertake the management of Wigmore Hall as a national and international centre for chamber music'. The precision of this definition may have come as a surprise to many. For decades, the Arts Council had never shown an interest in identifying or shaping Wigmore's artistic role. Perhaps they hoped Westminster City Council might fund a definition of role and purpose that ACE had signally failed to do.

Paula Best, a long-serving staff member from 1985, recalls that little changed in day-to-day practice under Westminster's control, but the first computers were installed, as was a computerized box-office system. The Hall was listed as just another 'venue for hire' in the Borough. People would ring up and ask to hire it for a dance. Staff had to explain that the Wigmore was a concert venue with fixed seating. What kind of a hall was it? Senior House Manager David King remembers, 'William had very little money to pay for concerts. Artistes wanted to come but we couldn't afford to pay them. Ticket prices were too cheap; there were no Friends nor fundraising activity. Ninety five percent of concerts were "hall hires" for "debuts or farewells". Very few people came to an actual concert for its own sake. Some came only once to support a friend.'

Looking back on her first recital in 1975, Dame Felicity Lott, the lyric soprano and trustee, recalled the air of sadness about the Hall in those days: 'I felt the ghosts of a lot of people who had given their debut recitals there and never returned again.' A kind of artistic funeral parlour perhaps? However, for the first time in its existence, an element of supervision entered Wigmore Hall's life: Lyne kept artistic control, Westminster applied local authority administrative rules and the Hall came under the formal control of a council committee. Local authorities are understandably highly financially risk adverse, artistic programming is intrinsically risk prone. This type of governance, with its tight financial controls, limited Lyne's ability to plan programmes and take financial risk. Some Westminster councillors, such as Alan Bradley (later a very helpful Lord Mayor), understood the organization they had adopted but even they could only provide support within the customary framework of council practices.

The decisive change that opened the door to a brilliant future for Wigmore came within three years of Westminster Council's takeover. Recognizing that an organization that provided arts sat uneasily in an authority delivering services, they announced that Wigmore would become an independent charity with its own board of trustees and some continuing financial support. Visionary and realistic as this was, Westminster went further by funding the renovation of the dingy, unusable basement of the Hall and making it suitable for catering, hospitality and events. The first stage of its modernization could take place.

After a 16-month closure, Wigmore Hall reopened in November 1992 with facilities more akin to those of any other modern arts venue. It was 'a new lease of life,' says David King, 'the next chapter in Wigmore's history.' When the independent charitable trust was formed in 1993, the Hall could seek freedom on its own terms rather than being a tiny part of a huge council. Nothing should take away from Westminster Council's vision in setting up Wigmore on generous terms. As an independent charity, Wigmore would have governance of a mature kind as never before: the Hall could build its own future and take responsibility for doing so.

Businessman Sir Trevor Holdsworth became the first chairman, forming a board which included Westminster Council representatives and major figures in the musical world, such as Sir John Tooley, former Director of the Royal Opera House. I was invited to join as I was known as a regular attendee (I stood down as trustee when I went to the Barbican in 1995). Governance was starting to take shape.

William Lyne felt strengthened by the board, who trusted him and did so in the perennially risky environment of programming and promoting concerts. He understood that they had only one priority: the health, wealth and prosperity of the Wigmore Hall. The importance of this new structure and relationship could not be overestimated. Of course, Lyne now had to answer to a board of expert outsiders but they could support and advise him and enable ambition to flourish in ways never previously conceivable. Yet there was a curious interim period in the fledgling board's early existence from 1993. Tony Allen, a senior accountant from Price Waterhouse Cooper, recalls what he saw as 'an interesting progression. Wigmore Hall was not yet in charge of its own destiny. It still felt "controlled" by Westminster City Council. William made the music his own. The Board discussed the management and organization but deferred to the Council. The new Board didn't quite know what it was doing in its own right.' It was as if neither could quite believe that the future truly lay in Wigmore's own hands. This was a reminder that boards and organizations must develop their own character when circumstances change.

In Tony Allen's account, the essential next step came when Trevor Holdsworth stepped down as chairman in 1998. I was approached to succeed him the following year and thought I could offer several advantages: I knew the Wigmore from my previous time as trustee, I knew William Lyne well, my wife and I came to almost as many concerts at Wigmore as we did at my home base, the Barbican. The musical interests of the two venues did not overlap. My years at the Barbican had given me a position in the music scene that could be used to the Hall's benefit. In 1999, I took over a going concern, with a great director, strong artistic programme, loyal audience and growing reputation. If, as Tony Allen recalls, Wigmore had yet to evolve into areas such as marketing and fundraising against a background of falling public funding, these seemed to me activities that would be rapidly learned and easily put into practice. But there was a lot to put in place.

As chairman, the most important part of my role was the relationship with the director. It was also the easiest part. I liked William Lyne as a person, admired him as an artistic director. We soon found that our judgements on performers were very close, often somewhat different from majority opinion. Usually we sat on seats just across the right-hand aisle in nearby rows. Comments, ideas, news or gossip were easily exchanged then as they were in the Green Room when congratulating performers after a concert. Some underestimated William because of his ready smile, warm Australian burr and apparently unassuming manner. This was foolish. Only the most resilient could have survived the years of oversight, indifference and neglect. It needed that doyen of artists' managers, Robert Rattray, to understand and express the nature of the tasks Lyne fulfilled and the qualities he possessed as a music professional: 'Never underestimate the suspicion of artists; never under-value the patience, vision and sheer exuberant professionalism required to put a season together; always keeping the best, delicately but ruthlessly expunging the "not quite good enough"; regularly reinventing yourself, always on the lookout for the new way of presenting the old and the new!'

It was a privilege for me to observe at close quarters what Rattray called William's 'tightrope act of astonishing versatility'. As well as this essential relationship with the chief executive, I stood ready to speak up for the Wigmore against critics, rivals or those of evil intent. Challenges would soon come from quite other directions.

If William Lyne was at the height of his powers, he may also have been close to their limit. Now in his seventies, he believed that the Hall's finances could only support the promotion of 95 concerts per year, the rest would be filled with 'hall hires' of varying quality. From this point of view, his vision was a restricted one. Physically, he found the myriad tasks of artistic planning and running a growing and increasingly complex organization more and more taxing. A mountain of paperwork would grow on his desk until it toppled to the floor under its own instability. 'Avalanche!' William would cry and the devoted team would rush in to pick up the chaos of papers. In his 37-year career at Wigmore, he had done literally everything from managing 'front of house' to shifting pianos – the more complex world now needed different solutions.

The trustees took the decision to split the director's job in two: the leadership would stay with the Artistic Director, the management and administration would be placed onto other shoulders. Such separation of responsibilities was familiar in the arts world. In December 2000, the trustees appointed a 28-year-old Irishman, John Gilhooly, as the new executive director. He had a good record as a manager; we may have underestimated at that time that he had a real musical background as well. What Gilhooly did not mention at interview was that he had known of the Wigmore Hall since the age of 11. The local Protestant Church of Ireland schoolmaster in the Irish town of Castle Connell, John Ruddock, was friendly with William Lyne. He would send performers eager for a trial run of a forthcoming Wigmore recital over to Ruddock for a rehearsal. In this way the 11-year-old Gilhooly heard and met great artists of the future such as the pianists András Schiff and Imogen Cooper and the clarinettist Michael Collins.

Gilhooly understood that he was a newcomer, an intruder possibly, into a tiny, close-knit group of people who had done artistic wonders over many years on minuscule resources. He had to earn not only Lyne's confidence but the trust of his right-hand staff, David King and Paula Best. His approach, he says, was based on listening, not moving too quickly and showing that change was possible and beneficial. He became part of what was still essentially 'a family'.

Lyne's departure from the directorship was only a matter of when, not whether. But his decision to retire in 2002 was, says Tony Allen, 'like a death in the family'. Though this was hardly a surprise, the trustees faced a major challenge. Should we try to find 'another William', identify a different kind of successor or reshape the management?

The plain fact was that you could not replicate him and the trustees should not have tried to do so. Tony Allen certainly believes that we weren't clear what we were looking for and did not examine alternatives sufficiently thoroughly. Hilary Browne-Wilkinson points out that the job description for the new director was built on the job that Lyne actually did. We had only divided that post in two – artistic and management – because William could not do both. She argues that the artistic directorship was not a big enough role in itself once Gilhooly was running the management. By trying to build a future job on a structure devised for a unique individual at a particular time, the trustees set up an inevitable tension between the artistic and administrative. There was, says Browne-Wilkinson, 'lack of clarity.' As chairman, I failed to lead the examination of alternatives or guide the board into serious discussion of alternatives.

As outgoing director, William Lyne did not find the business of appointing his successor easy. He wanted to sit on the interview panels, even have the final say on the appointment itself. In principle, I am wholly opposed to having the outgoing incumbent involved in finding their successor. We compromised: William's perspectives and judgement of people could be valuable, but he would not attend interviews. The trustees would make the final decision.

Lyne had a further suggestion: rather than look for an artistic director to lead the organization, recognize Gilhooly as chief executive and titular head and appoint an artistic director to support him; in other words, turn the existing leadership structure on its head. This was so far from my own thinking that, according to Gilhooly, I had rung him and advised him not to think of applying for the main job. I still think that was the right advice and the right decision. John was very young, he was learning on the job, and to have exposed him to the full responsibilities of leadership and a role in artistic planning would have been several challenges too far. It might even have damaged him.

The advertised job description contained the phrase that the candidate would be 'someone who would innovate based on a strong artistic tradition'. I had no doubts about what the words implied then or since. One candidate stood out above the others, a musician, scholar and writer, who came highly lauded by his employer, the Aldeburgh

Festival. Paul Kildea was an Australian in his mid-forties, with a strong, outgoing character and direct manner. Tony Allen recognized his vision, his energy, his sense of purpose and strategy. Hilary Browne-Wilkinson saw him as 'confident, very knowledgeable and seemed to be perceptive about the Hall'. John Gilhooly thought it 'seemed a really good choice because on paper, it was exactly what you had advertised for'. For my part, I liked his readiness to innovate, to push the Hall forward in new directions.

One trustee preferred another candidate judged to have a 'safe pair of hands'. That disagreement mattered less than the fact that this notoriously indiscreet trustee made it public to all and sundry. When another trustee joined in the criticism of the appointment, albeit for other reasons, we had that worst of situations, a board publicly known to be 'divided' over the key appointment and gossiping about it. As chairman, I never succeeded in silencing the gossip or unifying the board over Kildea's appointment.

I noted in the September 2003 edition of the Hall's annual record that Paul Kildea was always told that 'William Lyne is a hero and an impossible act to follow'. I urged him to 'fashion his own artistic profile and delight and stretch us'. Personally, I looked forward to a new, vigorous leader. Kildea could never complain of lack of support from his chairman but it turned out that Lyne was indeed an impossible act to follow.

Any Director of Wigmore Hall must align fully with the Three As – Artists, Agents, Audiences. Without this Triple A Rating no director could succeed. The new director was to lose the confidence of all three. Worse still, he never gained the support of the Wigmore 'family' – the small group of dedicated professionals who kept the place running under Lyne.

Among trustees too, first impressions were poor. The American trustee Cita Stelzer, a veteran of US arts boards, was quick to notice: 'He had no experience of managing board members. This was not the way the boards should be run. His manner was too casual. He assumed he could change everything the way he wanted.' Two essential constituencies of support, colleagues and trustees, were gone.

Almost certainly, Kildea had lost the Third A – the audience – before he even took up the post. In the months between appointment and taking up the job, Wigmore audience gossip was rife with Kildea's reported opinions. The Wigmore audience is easy to satirize as traditional, conventional, elderly and set in their ways. Even if a part of that were accurate, they are above all loyal, supportive, knowledgeable and not stupid, probably the Hall's secret weapon. Only a fool would alienate them; only someone with an exaggerated sense of their own superiority would patronize them; only the reckless would disregard them. Wigmore audiences talk, gossip and communicate because they care. They did not like what they heard of Paul Kildea from the start.

Paula Best believes he did not understand the importance of relationships with the audience. Kildea may have lost it irrevocably after a concert by the great Norwegian pianist Leif Ove Andsnes on 10 March, 2004. Present were the Hall's Patron, HRH The Duke of Kent, and the Hall's most generous and loyal financial donors, members of the Rubinstein Circle. When Andsnes appeared at the post-concert reception, Kildea's welcome praised him for being a 'clever bastard'. The shock was palpable, the offence huge, what was plain 'Aussie vernacular' detonating disastrously in a totally different culture and environment. Only someone with a tin ear for the nuances of culture and expression could have committed the error.

The following morning, Gilhooly's phone rang hot with voices of outrage, while I fielded the letters. Both of us defended Paul but the damage was being done. Standing front of house several nights a week, David King, an immediate point of contact for the audience, bore the brunt of their criticism. His own measured conclusion was that Kildea 'threw things out and this was too much of a shock for patrons. He wanted more contemporary music and didn't like Schubert! Had he done it more gradually, it might have worked. It was such a gear change. Audiences are creatures of habit.' Almost as an afterthought he added: 'Respect has to be earned, you can't rush it.' Sadly, Paul Kildea lost the Wigmore audience's respect before he had even earned it.

It was not long before he lost the two other parts of the Triple A Rating: artists and their agents. Artists thought the new director was trying to impose his views on what they should perform, while agents judged he was booking his friends and disregarding loyal and loved Hall artists. Some of the leading agents, people with decades of experience in artist management, broke off relations and made it clear privately why they were doing so. Artists declined to perform and were welcomed by rival venues. Perhaps most damaging of all, Kildea wanted to perform personally on the Wigmore stage. Seeing himself as a conductor, he devised programmes with himself in the principal role. David King says, 'It felt strange,' adding pithily, 'the Wigmore platform is there for the artistes not for your own promotion.' Many others were blunter: for the director to present himself as performer was just plain wrong.

While the observable and unpopular side of Kildea's direction drew the most criticism, box-office numbers were telling their own story. In the foyer, David King felt attendances ebbing: 'Paul had undone so much of the good work that William and we in his close team had built up over so many years.' The accountant trustee, Tony Allen, faced facts: 'The audience walked with its feet. Box office was bad. Kildea nearly lost us the Hall.' This was no exaggeration. So, when John Gilhooly as Executive Director presented financial numbers to trustees in Kildea's second year, an existing shortfall of £170K was forecast to become £250K by the end of the financial year. Most of this was due to falling attendances for the programming. Wigmore had no reserves to draw on; we faced a prospect of being 'trading insolvently'. Only the fact that Gilhooly was running the administration tightly and a fortuitous legacy of £250K from a loyal audience member saved us. In Aubrey Adams' judgement, we came through 'by the skin of our teeth'.

Clearly, the experiment of having a 'performer/director' had not worked. We had not advertised for it; as chairman, I failed to manage it. Kildea moved on in 2005. As I recorded in that year's edition of *The Score*, 'After two years with us, Paul Kildea felt that the conflict between the demands of artistic direction and his other performing and academic interests was going to prove increasingly hard to handle. In the circumstances, we all decided that a clear resolution before conflicts of interest appeared was in everyone's best interests.' It was the publisher-trustee Julia Macrae who pointed out that we had the answer to the succession standing in front of us. John Gilhooly had, after all, refurbished the Hall, led a capital campaign and was approved by William Lyne.

Gilhooly's initial appointment for a six-month interim period was a prudent insurance against possible error. In his recollection, when I phoned to appoint him as caretaker, I said, 'There's nothing as permanent as a temporary. Be ready to be interviewed.'

Before Wigmore Hall itself could move on as an organization, trustees and staff had to take a long hard look at the events of the previous two years. Opinions and judgements varied. Tony Allen thought the board should have 'picked up earlier what was going wrong'. For Hilary Browne-Wilkinson, it was 'a hiccough', for others, a necessary transition. For the American trustee, Cita Stelzer, the speed with which the board acted to resolve the situation was surprising, but rather satisfying, adding, 'It was done very quietly.'

From my point of view as the chairman throughout the time, many questions needed answering. Were the trustees too set on finding another William Lyne, a unique person who sprang from a unique set of circumstances? (Probably yes.) Did they explore the possibility of creating a new management structure sufficiently or indeed at all? (Certainly no.) Was the interview process sufficiently rigorous in questioning the candidate's lack of management experience? (Definitely no.) Did the interview adequately test the extent of the candidate's performing ambitions and the radicalism of his programming ideas? (Definitely no.) Perhaps most of all, how could the trustees have failed to assess the candidate's character? Later, colleagues spoke of Kildea's failure to consult, his lack of collegiality, his reluctance to recognize, according to David King, that he inherited a 'well-oiled machine, we knew how to deliver concerts'.

On the day that he left, Paula Best recalls a palpable sense of relief. The faces of staff 'were wreathed in smiles'. She herself no longer contemplated resigning from the job of her life and her love. Kildea had by then 'lost' the Wigmore audience, artistes, agents and staff. The 'Triple A Rating' had vanished. Were we, as trustees, sufficiently aware of what our staff felt? (Probably not.) I would add to this charge sheet of governance failure: how could we have failed to see some of the issues that lay beneath Kildea's confidence and energy?

For all these failures, I may have been quite the wrong chairman for the radical new director. In my executive roles at BBC World Service and the Barbican I had put rapid change and innovation into practice. While I often cautioned Paul Kildea in private, a different chairman, less wedded to the desirability of change, might have handled him better, but as one close colleague observed, 'He was the main author of his own downfall.'

Nothing could excuse the list of governance failures set out earlier or my own involvement in them. Once the parting of the ways was agreed with Kildea, the next trustee meeting interviewed John Gilhooly for the post of director after a six-month interim and appointed him to the reunified position. I then offered the board my resignation and left the room. When the trustees called me back, they said they did not think my resignation was necessary and did not accept it. Aubrey Adams, a trustee and later the chairman, says, 'It may have been the honourable thing to do, but actually it was not the best thing to do, unless there was a fault in the process of choosing him. There was proper process, he was generally accepted as being the right choice and it went wrong.'

If my perhaps self-indulgent resignation offer made me feel better, it might have damaged the Wigmore. The possible consequences of offering to resign just when we had appointed a new, young director never crossed my mind. As John Gilhooly recalls the occasion: 'I remember being taken aback and thinking, "Well, that's not a good way to start." It would have done huge damage to the organization, had you gone.' Fortunately, the trustees took a longer view. Quite rapidly as Gilhooly showed himself increasingly sure-footed as director, perspectives began to change. Tony Allen reflected: 'John wasn't ready to be a candidate when William retired. He grew into his role. He had time to mature to take on the full role when he did.' In other words, the previous two years could be seen as a blessing in disguise. Now, the leadership of Wigmore was unified again: there was only one director.

Trustees noticed the difference immediately. For Cita Stelzer, when Gilhooly became director, 'Everything changed. I don't know how he did it. He was careful, nuanced, terrific. John Gilhooly was "a gift from heaven". He respected William Lyne and the institution. He told the board everything. He was feeling his way when he began. He didn't jump in when he wasn't ready.' Audiences came back. Loyalty to the Hall and its music ran strong.

This loyalty had been nurtured over several years with an increasingly confident approach to fundraising or 'development'. Management had used the 1991–92 closure to start a Friends' Membership scheme. It attracted growing support. With a new development manager, the experienced Marie-Helene Osterweil, the year 2001 saw both a Gala Evening and a major Centenary Year concert of the highest ambition and quality. The audience not only bought tickets but seemed ready to respond to further appeals for their support. The basic Friends scheme had already been reinforced by a 'higher level' group called the Rubinstein Circle. Founded by the devoted, demanding but dynamic trustee Jackie Rosenfeld, she led by example with a £5,000 gift for one recital. Rubinstein Circle members were asked to give the significant sum of £2,000 per year to belong. Jackie believed in both giving and asking. She was a fundraising leader. Modest benefits and advantages were attached to membership. But that most trustees and a useful number of the audience were ready to support Wigmore's activity over and above the large number of tickets they bought was a reassuring indicator.

Osterweil saw her first task as being 'to reinforce Wigmore Hall as a registered charity, as a trust that relied on philanthropy.' Audiences required reminding that the Hall needed money to present the music everyone loved, and that it was possible to give. First, the Hall had to develop the habit of asking and finding the best ways to 'make the ask in order to encourage giving'. Before that strategy could be put into effect, the trustees endured two false starts over the best way to drive giving. The first involved setting up a Development Sub-Committee chaired by a board member, Hilary Browne-Wilkinson. The second, quite separate, initiative was less important but failing to manage it proved a distraction. Most arts organizations at the time had 'American Friends' groups. That surely was the development 'crock of gold' at the end of the rainbow of goodwill spanning the Atlantic. Neither project worked as freestanding entities. The answer was simple. As John

Gilhooly observed, 'Parallel boards don't work particularly in a small organization.' But if they were set up, they had to be integrated into the board governance structure. It was my responsibility as chairman to organize the integration and I failed to see that it was needed or how it might be done at all.

Fortunately, the relationship with the audience was not damaged. There were major projects to move towards: the long overdue refurbishment of the auditorium and the public spaces, and the purchase of the lease of the Wigmore Hall itself. The story is simply stated. In 2003–04, the Wigmore raised £3.4 million for the refurbishment of the entire venue, a figure previously regarded as inconceivably ambitious. In the September 2005 edition of *The Score*, I was able to note that the project had come in 'on cost and on time'; it left no 'capital overhang' and delivered everything promised, from better seats, better sight lines, air conditioning, lighting and greatly improved dining and public venues. As well as major charitable donors, the Wigmore 'family' had given in extraordinary numbers. The person responsible for delivering the appeal, Marie-Helene Osterweil concluded: 'We raised the money, we did what we did, we did it in the time that we said and we did it to the fullest.' And the professional fundraiser knew she had won something almost more precious: 'We had a donor base that we could really work with.' In the sometime arcane world of fundraising one truth is universally recognized: those who give once usually give again.

The success of the project gave us confidence to launch a further appeal for £3.1 million to buy the lease of the Hall just six years later. Owning our lease would directly save us £140K per year in rent and protect us from potentially ruinous rent increases in future years. This appeal succeeded too. As Gilhooly observed: 'The audiences saw the money that would have been spent on rent immediately pumped into the programming.' Today, the Wigmore presents no fewer than 400 concerts a year as 'own promotions', a step change from the 95 of the Lyne years. Trust was reinforced as promises were made good. The board too learned how the 'giving' relationship worked. As Tony Allen observed: 'We only became aware of how much the audience loved the Hall when we started asking for money. Asking for money was part of growing up from Westminster City Council.' Building on these successes, the Wigmore could start looking to secure its future by launching an appeal for legacies – this too did not fall on deaf ears.

There is a puzzle here. Given the drama and turmoil of many of the years in which money was successfully raised for major projects, why did board and leadership turbulence not undermine the giving? One explanation is that most audience members knew nothing of such disputes and only a very few cared. Governance does matter but its workings at strategic level are distant from buying a ticket and enjoying a concert. But something deeper was firmly in play. Audiences knew year by year that almost every night and sometimes twice a day, music would be made on the Wigmore stage at the highest level. As David King said: 'It is the best place to hear music in London. We are very good at understanding people. It didn't happen overnight. Find out what they want and give them more. What we do, we do very well.' Yet, part of the puzzle remains. Not long ago the Wigmore Hall might have been dismissed as 'an old-fashioned hall, with an old-fashioned audience, listening to an old-fashioned repertoire'. Some thought it so, others believed it. Some didn't care if it survived or vanished. A few thought they could take it on, steal the artistes and compete but they failed. Today, the Hall is the same but handsomely refurbished; the acoustic is the same; the core repertoire remains but is carefully extended; the core audience lives, moves on, but has been extended to include the young. So, how has this formula for success been achieved?

Wigmore's success has been built on 10 principles and practices. Never codified or expressed in formal terms, they may even be the stronger for being implicit. They were certainly not an accident. John Gilhooly stood firm on the Hall's artistic vision: it never dumbed down its programming, never compromised, never abandoned its core audience, did not indulge in audience segmentation and market analysis, valued and nurtured its artistes, stayed true to excellence, built alliances, placed its experience at the service of the musical world, kept up with the times without losing its foundations in tradition. There may have been an eleventh principle observed in practice: trustees never interfered with the director's artistic decisions.

Does this suggest that the 'tightrope' that William Lyne was famously said to have walked was still being traversed? Rather, his successor John Gilhooly actually made the crossing to the other side and was creating his own vision in his own landscape. The one-time successor had become a leader in his own right.

Gilhooly's astute combination of the mainstream with the less expected underpinned by performance excellence was built on two foundations. The first was the relationship between the Hall and the audience which he understood from the beginning: 'It's got to be personal. It goes back to the ownership thing. The sense of ownership from the audience and those who want to help us, the sense of connection with managers here, that's what generates gifts. Trust in the future.'

The second pillar of his and the Hall's success was the trustee board. From the beginning, the American trustee, Cita Stelzer, recognized its character: 'It was good, terrific. I would give it 9.7/10. It was a small board, unlike those big US boards where people can pay to get on. It was dedicated to what it did. It was never social, never *Tatler*.' Tony Allen agreed that the board was the right size for a charity responsible for the institution but not answerable to it. Better still, it was never driven by concerns about wealth or social position: 'You did not have to put money in. Everybody on the board did give but no one talked about it, whatever they gave.' To this day, chairman Aubrey Adams, with long experience of the commercial world, believes that for a charity, the small Wigmore board 'was a governance board of the right size, not made up of people who have got lots of money and saying, "Fine, you want to be on the board, sign the cheque"'. It was never the chairman's role to lead the development activity, they have other responsibilities to fulfil. Too many boards fail to recognize the difference.

One further characteristic of the Wigmore board deserves mention: every member loved music, every member attended concerts, no one tried to interfere in the programming of the music or choice of the performers (they had opinions but only as any member of the audience). The regular, visible presence of board members at concerts provided a continuum of trust, an immediacy of communication that could be special to Wigmore. It amounted to a feature, a vital aspect of its governance.

It is universally agreed that the relationship between chair and chief executive is the key to good governance. Viewing my own record, I believe that I worked well with William Lyne; that I may have been too close to Paul Kildea but acted swiftly to conclude a relationship that was not working; and that apart from one period when I left him unprotected from possible interference, John Gilhooly and I worked in the closest possible harmony.

Gilhooly himself describes our chairman/chief executive interaction over a decade in this way: 'There was almost daily contact, even for two minutes. I was on the phone to you to wave red flags, to put the board in a position to know. If there was a crisis, real or imaginary, you were very good at handling this. Sometimes I was wrong and things didn't happen. I always had the trust to go to you and say, "I think this could go wrong".

My own image of the heart of Wigmore governance is that of Gilhooly and me sitting in adjacent rows on the right-side aisle of the Hall and exchanging comments, ideas, thoughts and, very importantly for me, gossip from the musical world. We were happy to be at Wigmore Hall. That was the personal and practical side of effective governance. It might not be in the textbooks, but it cannot be overestimated.

REFLECTIONS

Every organization is better off with a system of governance. Bad governance holds an organization back, but can be remedied. No governance stops an organization from moving forward; that cannot be put right.

A local authority, however well-intentioned, is not a suitable vehicle for managing an arts institution.

Even lacking governance support or financial backing, an arts institution can achieve something, provided it is based on vision.

When a charismatic, long-serving leader retires, expect the need for a transition. Trustees should take time to examine all the choices before them, nothing should be ruled out.

The departing leader should generally not be involved in choosing the successor.

Avoid trying to replicate the outgoing leader, however attractive that may seem – it is almost certainly impossible anyway.

A successor to the leadership position is unlikely to be identified in a single interview. Take time to examine the candidate deeply. The consequences of a decision taken in an hour or two will live with you for years: 'Appoint in haste, repent at leisure'.

If the right candidate does not emerge at first interviews, do not appoint someone who seems good enough – you will regret it. Instead, conduct another search, six months later. It's amazing how the field of applicants can change in that time.

You cannot support a new appointment too closely in the first six months. If an appointment is not working, act speedily to agree on a change.

Offering your resignation may satisfy your own feelings but think of the consequences on others first.

Any new governance body will take time to find its voice. Freedom to imagine carries responsibility for the consequences.

If you need to raise money, you must dare to ask first.

Do not underestimate the readiness of the audience to do more than buy tickets.

Unless the audience trusts you, they will not support you.

Supporters who give will usually give again. Do not be surprised.

If you raise money for a capital project, make sure what is promised is delivered to the letter.

Fundraising is best done by a committee separate from but linked into the main board.

Never undervalue the audience that you have, nor imagine the audience you do not have is bigger, better, richer and somehow more desirable.

Do not abandon what you stand for and are good at. Extend and build on the base that you have.

Do not believe that marketing can find better answers than vision and core principles.

Keeping in close touch with the audience is a big part of good governance.

A good board need not be a big board. An effective board is not defined by whether its members give financially or not. A really good board gives but does not talk about it. Also, a good board is not a social board.

A chairman is not principally a fundraiser, or at all. They are there to ensure board cohesion and to fulfil its charitable responsibilities, such as solvency.

A chairman and director will talk every day and chat most evenings. A chairman will let a director down on occasion but should not do so too often.

6

University of the Arts London (UAL): Unity from Diversity (2007–2013)

Interviews with

Lorraine Baldry, Chair, Finance Committee, Governor, 2008–19

Stephen Barter, Deputy Chair, Chair, Finance Committee, Member Estates
  Committee, Governor, 1998–2009

Sir Nigel Carrington, Rector, later Vice-Chancellor, 2008–2020

Michael Cassidy, City Leader, Governor, 1997–2006

Clara Freeman, Deputy Chair, Governor, 2002–14

David Lindsell, Chair Audit Committee, Governor, 2011–present

Stephen Marshall, University Secretary, 2008–present

Grayson Perry, Artist, Governor, 2010–15, Chancellor, 2006–present

Will Wyatt, Chair Court of Governors, 1999–2007

A chance meeting at a pedestrian crossing by the Smithfield meat market
in the City of London in the summer of 2006 would have a big effect on
my next involvement in governance. Will Wyatt and I were old colleagues

from the BBC, though his background in BBC Television, where he had been managing director, and my own at BBC World Service meant that we had never worked together closely. During our pavement exchanges, he explained that he was chairman of what had formerly been the 'London Institute', a loose gathering of five major London art colleges. This had just become a fully-fledged university, the University of the Arts London (UAL). Wyatt had also established an ambitious new campus for Chelsea College of Art on the grounds of the former Army Hospital at Millbank. With an even more ambitious building project at King's Cross in view, he decided to stand down after eight years as chairman. The single Chelsea campus had involved a daring property deal, selling four scattered college premises adjacent to the King's Road. The mastermind of that property consolidation was Michael Cassidy, my former chairman at the Barbican Centre, whom I admired and had worked well with. I knew Michael to be a 'doer'. Suddenly, the University of the Arts London looked an interesting organization to be involved in once I finished my contract at the Barbican.

After a series of meetings with university governors and the university rector, the high-powered former civil servant Sir Michael Bichard, I was invited to be the next Chair of the Court of Governors, starting in March 2007. It would be a new experience in the fields of governance and fitted well with my departure from the Barbican later that summer. Within weeks, these plans nearly collapsed. My personal ambition was the cause. The university's governance was to be my saviour.

Undue ambition had led me to apply for the Chairmanship of the Trustees of the Victoria and Albert Museum (V&A). I was appointed in June 2007. Three weeks later, Stephen Barter, Deputy Chair of the UAL Governors, invited me in 'for a natter'. They were worried that in wearing two hats, there would be conflicts of interest between my roles at V&A and the University, not least over raising development funds. Worse still, they assumed UAL would lose out. In facing and raising such a sensitive question, the governors acted speedily, bravely and realistically. They knew that I might choose the 'glamour' of the V&A rather than the unknowable satisfactions of a fledgling university and preferred to face up to the potential conflict immediately rather than discover at a later stage that their new chairman was in fact riven and conflicted between his two roles. It cannot have been easy for the UAL governors but in acting as they did, they faced up to their governance responsibilities full-on. The following day, I told them I would stay on as UAL chair and withdraw from my chairmanship of the V&A.

The three-year-old University of the Arts London was a curious but interesting confection. When the Inner London Education Authority (ILEA) was wound up in 1990, the future of London's celebrated arts colleges was a serious problem. Their names and alumni amounted to a roll call of the nation's artistic creativity – Central Saint Martins, Chelsea, Camberwell. Under the general rubric of 'creativity' and administrative tidiness, the London College of Fashion and London College of Printing (now the London College of Communication) were thrown in with the art colleges. From 1989, all five colleges, whatever their exact disciplines, came under a single governance structure, a governing body, a full Court of Governors. They were in truth odd bedfellows, producing great artists and designers at one end, smart fashion, training tailors and printers at the other – almost everything from high-level creation to routine vocation. Some called it the 'British Leyland' of the artistic world, evoking the botched automotive conglomerate, where job lots of failing motor car brands were thrown together in a desperate effort to save them.

In 1975, British Leyland had collapsed in a morass of mediocrity. By contrast, within just over two decades, UAL's Court of Governors transformed what started as a bureaucratic convenience into one of the leading centres for arts and creativity in the world. Governance was the driver of change. It might not have been predicted, it could not have been guaranteed; its success should not be underestimated.

The real impetus started with Will Wyatt's appointment as Chair of Governors in 1999. His recollection is that the five colleges were dragged 'kicking and screaming' into their new entity. Each believed their qualities were not just special but unique. All treasured their historic independence, ignoring the reality that each was too small to survive in a new, globalized education world. Wyatt found 'a confederacy of colleges who didn't always like each other or want anyone else to succeed'. In practice, what individual colleges wanted came first and with some luck and wheeler-dealing, they might occasionally agree on policies in the interests of all. Stephen Barter, later Deputy Chair, observed: 'A loose affiliation of similar-minded individuals who happened to fall under one umbrella. Great credence was given to the wishes of the colleges. The rector had to be careful how he exercised his authority.' Bluntly, the status quo came first with financial viability an overriding priority.

Within two years, Wyatt took the opportunity of the retirement of the rector to put in a leader of his own choice: 'I felt what was required was a strong leader who would take no prisoners in continuing to modernize.' He found the person he wanted in Sir Michael Bichard, Permanent Secretary to the Department of Education, with a reputation as a high-level Whitehall fixer. Staff would have liked an academic as rector, but the governors made the selection. Wyatt fed in Bichard's name as a late entrant while promising him nothing more than serious consideration for his candidacy. Not for the last time in UAL's history, the 'lay' governors were the radical force with a more dynamic idea of the University's potential than the academics. Governors recognized Bichard as a 'major player' and appointed him in 2001. He lived up to his reputation as a doer. There was a lot to be done to turn this loose and reluctant confederation into an institution with a sense of cohesion and integrity, one which was greater than the sum of its parts. Indeed, there were years of 'kicking and screaming' to come.

It was good fortune that UAL had two governors with huge experience of property on the court – Stephen Barter, a real estate professional, and Michael Cassidy, a City of London Councilman of 40 years' standing. Property decisions became the galvanizer of change and the University's direction. Good fortune played its part as well. As Cassidy recalls it, the University had a long lease on a building in the middle of Long Acre, just off London's Leicester Square, just as it was beginning its transformation into a prime retail area. The owner, resident in Monaco, was dying and wanted to settle his affairs. He named a price of £11 million for the freehold. The University, says Cassidy, 'got their act together and bought it within 10 days.' More amazingly still, 'We applied to Westminster Council to change the planning permission from education to shopping and within two or three months had sold the building to the retailer H&M for £22 million.' At that stage, the court, says Cassidy, 'had no idea what value they were sitting on.' The Long Acre property sale was the wake-up call to what might be possible.

Many university governing bodies would have pocketed the windfall and frittered it away on routine expenditures. The UAL Court suddenly realized the strategic value of its plethora of scattered properties. They would not sit there, ignore the money – in effect, an endowment – and have no ambitions for it. There was one opportunity very close by. In Chelsea, says Barter, the College owned a 'very fragmented estate scattered over four sites'. Putting them on the market as a single investment opportunity, according to Cassidy, made it 'a very, very attractive investment' for major developers. So it proved with the University collecting close to £100 million for the deal. This was not a university being turned into a property company by ruthless businessmen – these were expert governors deploying their property skills in the interest of the University. They conjured an overriding institutional and academic vision, a historic opportunity: to house the entire Chelsea College on its own single-site campus on Millbank, adjacent to Tate Britain.

The problem, according to the chair, Will Wyatt, was a certain entrenched conservatism among teaching staff. Chelsea academic staff liked being where they were in four separate buildings, four separate schools: 'They had their own cultures, but they were cultures that often hid themselves away. People on the "foundation course" rarely saw anybody from any other part of the college, let alone the rest of the University.' How they could create an effective arts institution from scattered premises is impossible to understand.

Wyatt's own very different and passionately held vision was 'in the creative world, creative people strike sparks off each other. If you're all on one campus, you bump into inspiring people and find opportunities for ideas.' Chelsea academics did not share the vision and 'put up a hell of a lot of resistance.' Despite this, the single campus on Millbank was bought and built, and Chelsea College could start a new part of its history. An artistic and academic vision rooted in the practicalities of property deals and the business of making money was the creation of the Court of Governors. When it came to having a vision for their college, let alone the University, academic staff proved myopic, lacking the necessary skillset. The successful establishment of Chelsea College campus in 2005 gave UAL the confidence that consolidation of its more than 20 properties scattered all over London had to be the way ahead. A strategic direction was set; its actual and symbolic importance for UAL's future cannot be overstated.

The University also was systematic in its approach to succession planning. I followed Will Wyatt into the Chair of the Court in March 2007. Will had persuaded Bichard to remain for a year under a new chairman so that the latter could appoint the person he or she wanted to work with. Such an approach may have been ordinary good practice but its orderliness paid off. By the time the search for a successor to the rectorship started, I had had a year to get to know the needs and workings of the University at first hand.

The selection process was nothing if not thorough to the point of being protracted. The court delegated the task to a subgroup led by me and Clara Freeman, a governor with wide experience of personnel practices. The contracted headhunters, Odgers Berndtson, produced a strong but manageably-sized shortlist of candidates, almost all of them names known in the arts world. This was reassuring in itself: leading UAL was an attractive proposition to highly talented people. As Clara Freeman recalls it, the court subgroup interviewed all six on the shortlist. According to one candidate, 'It was a very big and serious interview, not at all cosy, very polite but very rigorous, very structured. I felt I had been put through my paces in my professional life, my private sector life, my interest in the arts and my knowledge of universities.'

Armed with this knowledge the subgroup interviewed a much shorter list. Clara Freeman and I then saw each applicant at Clara's home. We felt we were getting closer to a choice but wanted to make absolutely sure of our judgement. By this stage, according to one candidate, 'It was a more engaged process, more challenging and very charmingly interrogatory.' Clara wanted reassurance that everyone understood that the rectorship was a full-time post, involving a commitment to many evenings at University events.

After the final interviews, we knew that we had a real choice of two strong candidates before us. We chose Nigel Carrington, former managing partner of a huge law firm, Baker McKenzie, with a fascinating CV. Carrington then became Managing Director of McLaren Group, of which DaimlerChrysler AG was the largest shareholder. He followed this up with a Graduate Diploma in the History of Art at the Courtauld Institute. This was an impressive demonstration of a wide range of interests and many relevant skills. We liked the fact that he had experience in leading individuals who could not be bossed about, his approach to leadership was collegiate but firm. His personal manner was open, friendly, reasonable, even charming, and there was no doubt about his ability to put change into practice.

Carrington himself was well aware that taking a major position in an entirely new sector was a big personal risk, 'because of the culture clash of bringing in a private sector person to a university culture and a fear that academics always have that somebody coming in from the private sector will change the underlying values of the university.' He was appointed in January 2008.

University staff were not involved in the selection process. In part, this was because of the need to protect the confidentiality of public and high-profile candidates. But it was also due to near-certainty that staff would have lobbied for an academic candidate especially as successor to a civil servant. Excellent as they were academically, they were not seen as the best judges of the wider interests of the University. Any debate would have been pointless. Besides, responsibility for the appointment lay with the governors, who were not inclined to shirk in their duties.

As a governance responsibility, the intensive selection process paid off. From Carrington's point of view, 'I felt I had been tested not only on my interest in the job but on my experience on how I would do it.' He added: 'The process was very professional. Of course, if it hadn't been professional, I probably would have been put off.'

From 2008, UAL had a new leadership team, that crucial chairman/ chief executive relationship. Carrington and I would be very different from the Wyatt/Bichard duo. With Wyatt coming from what he called the 'softer' world of broadcasting and Bichard from the 'sharp edge of tough government', they provided a strong contrast. This had been deliberate on Will Wyatt's part. He had precisely calibrated this interplay of their characters when he identified Bichard as his candidate for Rector: 'Michael's style was pretty upfront. He didn't just say it, he would do it.

I knew he would drive changes through. He was tough-minded and not afraid to be confrontational.' The two stood, Wyatt insists, 'shoulder-to-shoulder. He would push things through, I produced a slightly calming element.' In Stephen Barter's view, 'Bichard was sensitive and smart enough to understand the kind of organization he was dealing with, but there was a purpose and an objective and he got on with it.'

Wyatt described his own style as 'not particularly confrontational. I like to achieve what I can achieve by other means. I could charm senior staff, build trust so they thought "at least one of them is not a bastard trying to do us all down".' Wyatt saw himself as 'the acceptable face of necessary and unavoidable change'. This balance worked well – a rector who led and acted, a chair who conciliated and reassured. 'Push forward from the Rector, pull back from the Chair' would be one way of describing it. Each played their part.

If, as it turned out, Nigel Carrington and I were to work the other way round – an impatient chair, a more considered rector – that only showed there is no right formula for this crucial relationship. Each approach was shaped by and suited to the personalities involved.

In under 20 years, London's art colleges had undergone major change from freestanding institutions supervised by local government to a loose confederation where their independence reigned supreme to a university where they had to come to terms with an increasingly coherent centre. Carrington and I inherited a strong legacy from the Wyatt/Bichard years: a basically well-run administration, solvency without riches, the addition of a sixth college – Wimbledon – one striking new campus – Chelsea – and the prospect of an even more dramatic one, that for Central Saint Martins at King's Cross. Opportunities abounded; consistency of leadership and continuity of policies was possible.

Problems existed too. In my assessment, the University had a weak identity externally, it lacked cohesion internally, the traditional primacy of colleges once considered beyond challenge now needed direct confrontation. The University had to have a unity, to be a university in more than name.

First and foremost, Nigel Carrington and I were united in dismay at the way the Court of Governors worked. I was shocked at the numbers present at the quarterly meetings: chairman, 16 external governors, rector, deputy rector, four heads of college, four administrative heads including finance, four chosen by academic staff, one chosen by students. In practice, staff governors often found it hard to take university interests into account rather than acting as 'representatives' of their community. But sheer numbers were the problem. David Lindsell, Chair of the Audit Committee, observed: 'I have always had trouble with the size of the board, from 25 to well over 30. The more people there are on it, the less sense of individual responsibility there is.'

For Carrington, after the severe practicalities of a law firm, he 'was shocked, absolutely shocked, by the volume of paper, a splurge of mindless detail, not properly focussed. I had never encountered so much paper. You couldn't often detect any underlying strategic intent.' This was not the only institution where the quantities of information provided were designed not to illuminate but to confuse, not to assist governors to scrutinize but to prevent them from questioning effectively, not to facilitate accountability but to prevent it. If 'information is power', it must be remembered that 'too much information is a smokescreen'.

As a result of the numbers of people present at court meetings, the weight of academic staff, the volume of indigestible paper, external governors were and felt squashed. As chair, I felt impotent, ineffectual and frustrated. The Court of Governors, the constitutional centre of the university, was subjected to speeches by heads of college and university officers stating in effect that everything was fine, they knew more and they knew best. What could external governors say? In Lorraine Baldry's experience the presence of so many executives, 'closed down discussion. They were averse to it. That is always the danger when you bring in executives.' Registrar and Secretary Stephen Marshall noted, 'Governors felt the Court was swamped with executive officers who were in defensive mode the whole time.'

Worst of all, the trade union staff governor ignored my invitation to address university interests as a whole and subjected the court to extended harangues on trade union minutiae as if it were a union branch meeting. After a few such occasions I had a furious row with him at Court. I regretted losing my temper but learned later that my angry response had its impact. But if that was the way the University Court of Governors was supposed to go about its business, governance was a mess.

This was not just my view. As Carrington observed, 'There was a wholly dysfunctional relationship between the court and the executive. Court didn't feel they had access to all the drivers that shaped the University's position, either financially or academically.' It was, he concluded, an impossible situation: 'you couldn't really be a well-informed governing body because you wouldn't penetrate it all unless you had the time and patience to read, probably, a thousand pages.' How could I persuade distinguished outsiders to join the court to waste their time with such nonsense? Why should any busy professional come on board to endure this?

Within months of my becoming chairman, two incidents revealed where power was assumed to lie in the University. When the officer with overall responsibility for finance noted in a budget paper presented to the court that several million pounds of savings had to be found, I suggested ways in which budget holders should be questioned in order to release those savings. In Nigel Carrington's recollection, the officer, 'basically told you to take a running jump. She didn't want governors to understand the detail or to get involved in final strategy.' Other governors observed a 'reluctance to disclose, a discomfort at being cross-examined'. Carrington's own experience with the administration was if possible even worse than mine. When he decided to visit the University's scattered property domain of no fewer than 22 buildings, he was told he couldn't go unaccompanied since the Head of Estates reported to the Head of Corporate Resources. They would all visit together, or by implication, not visit at all.

If my priority was to make governance work, Nigel Carrington had to reform how the University was run, breaking the tight, local authority approach to information, control and power. We had parallel, urgent and connected agendas for action. Nigel wanted details of finance and administration to improve the flow of information. Only then could he supply the soon-to-be slimmed down court with what we needed to make good decisions. He brought his instincts and practices from previous lives into the academic world despite the fact that, 'many vice-chancellors, certainly at the time, advised me that the worst thing I could do was to get too close to the governing body'. After ignoring that cynical advice, he got close to the court, stayed close and worked in partnership with us. It proved to be the key to UAL's success.

That partnership began with our own relationship. Nigel and I met regularly on a monthly basis and saw one another frequently in between times. Our agreed *modus operandi* was 'You will always hear it from me first'. It was never breached. At an early meeting, I raised the subject of the clumsiness of the unwieldy gathering that the court was. External governors could not supervise if court meetings were dominated by the executive. This turned governance on its head. In future, only the rector, the registrar, staff governors, student and union representatives would attend automatically. Heads of colleges and other senior executives would attend only when business demanded. The secretary, Stephen Marshall, with experience of working in five universities, concluded tersely, 'There's no academic rationale for having the full executive team around the table.'

Excluding the heads of college and most executives from Court was crucial to the way its effectiveness blossomed thereafter. I did not feel they were in any sense excluded – they had no constitutional right to be there. The expertise and skills of governors could be engaged, their judgements and opinions heard, a feeling of cohesion achieved, a sense of purpose created. Powerful committee chairs such as Stephen Barter (Finance and later, Lorraine Baldry), John Parmiter (Estates), David Lindsell (Audit) and Clara Freeman (Personnel) not only established strong supervision of those activities but came together in a Chairman's Committee which took more routine matters off the front end of the court agenda. It would be too much to claim that these processes were streamlined but they certainly enabled the court to conduct orderly, strategic and effective supervision of university business.

Every few months, Nigel and I performed a ritual dance over the 'exclusion' of heads of college from Court of Governors' meetings. They were, he reported, very unhappy: could they come back? They had asked him to raise it with me, he had promised to do so and would I think again? I thanked him for informing me of their feelings but the slimmed-down court was working very well, I believed, and I would never go back to the old ways. I had indeed thought again and my answer was still 'no'. Nigel and I smiled; formalities had been observed and we moved on to other matters. In any case, by introducing a system where individual governors were linked to specific colleges for a year, by termly sandwich lunches at colleges, heads probably had more contact with the chair and governors than attending Court would have given them. Although I had the greatest respect and admiration for the skills and personalities of college heads, I just did not see their presence at Court as contributing to the University's effectiveness: Court is after all a supervisory body, not a representative body.

The reformed court allowed us to encourage a variety of useful outsiders onto it, knowing their time would not be wasted. One such individual was the artist, Grayson Perry. He would be a voice of the arts community but I also knew him as a person of great common sense and practicality. Why an artist of such standing would want to give up his precious creative time for the dubious pleasures of university governance was not clear. He explained that he was 'fascinated with the backstage. What did power look like in operation and in person?' Boards, he decided, needed a mixture of experience and skills, 'and a bit of spice'. Perhaps that would be his role. Yet he wondered what influence he could have: 'I felt like a seagull flapping at the *Titanic*. You squawk as much as you like but the ship won't change course. You need to shit in the Captain's eye.' Ultimately, Grayson was as active and constructive a governor as I expected.

A deeper and perhaps surprising result of giving governors the authority that was properly theirs was, as Lorraine Baldry recalled, 'We had a bit of fun as well. The important bit about any group of people who meet on a regular basis is that you're pleased to see some of them around the table.' Dinners, degree day ceremonies and sandwich lunches at individual colleges cemented governor relationships. For Lorraine, 'Governors had an opportunity to be part of something quite big and enjoyable and in the main, they took the opportunity.' Carrying out the necessary functions of governance did not have to be gloomy and austere. Far better done in an atmosphere of comradeship and conviviality, there were never factions or secret cabals on the court as a result.

Nigel Carrington himself took two early and decisive steps to make his mark and establish his authority. He told me that he would not take a salary increase in his first three years while parts of the University were undergoing restructure – he would not be seen as doing better than staff at such a time. This struck me as very astute. The court would not lose control nor be seen to lose control over the rector's remuneration at a time when several other universities throughout the UK took to over-rewarding their vice-chancellors, causing internal controversy and drawing external condemnation.

His second step was to cut out an entire senior layer of administration. It stood in his way, clogged up the flow of information and denied him contact with those that he felt he needed: 'If you're running a big law firm, you have unlimited liability for the debts of the partnership. You don't delegate decisions to people you don't talk to regularly.' The existing structure, the added senior layer, denied him access to people and detail he regarded as essential to reaching strategic conclusions. When he told me and Clara Freeman, by then the vice-chair, of his dramatic and daring plan to remove three of the most senior administrators, the logic behind it seemed beyond question. At a stroke, the bureaucracy would feel lighter, less oppressive, the flow of information from executive to governors likely to be freer, the network of relationships at the top of the institution closer and more direct.

Clara and I questioned Nigel about the need for such a daring upheaval, about the risks of implementing it and the opportunities that he foresaw. It never occurred to us to advise him not to act or to delay or implement by stages or over time; these were classic bureaucratic delaying tactics that would have negated the effect of what he needed to do. Court backed him; restructuring took place; all the benefits he hoped for occurred and sheer energy was released in an administration previously encumbered by too many layers.

Carrington's clarity of analysis and the determination of its execution had a further major, if perhaps unintended consequence: it totally stymied the staff unions. As changes elsewhere in the University were introduced, nobody could accuse the rector – later to be renamed vice-chancellor – of looking after his own financial interests first. As staff numbers were reduced and posts closed, unions could not claim that the lowest-paid were bearing the burden of savings. Those had started at the very top of the organization. In acting as he did, Nigel Carrington had simply shot the unions' fox. That wasn't why he acted; the changes needed to be made, their impact was large. Shrewdly and symbolically, he dispensed with the rector's driver. When he visited colleges arriving by tube, rucksack slung over his shoulder, staff noticed.

The main opportunity we inherited from the Wyatt/Bichard years was of another major campus consolidation to follow on from the one at Chelsea, that of perhaps the most celebrated institution of the University: Central Saint Martins. Formed of two colleges as its name made clear, the art college was a long walk between the two buildings in Charing Cross Road and Southampton Row. Many functions were duplicated as a result, there could be no feeling of a campus and Saint Martins retained a strong, possibly justified feeling, of its uniqueness. Both buildings were old, inefficient, ramshackle and crying out for renovation that was unaffordable. When in the 1990s the property developers Argent produced a plan for developing the huge empty spaces north of King's Cross, neglected by others for decades, spaces that were derelict, moribund if not actually dangerous, UAL persuaded them, as Stephen Barter recalls, that 'to have a university as an anchor with 5,000 students arriving, all hungry and thirsty, would have a multiplier effect on the whole location.' It would also be a physical centrepiece.

In presenting the proposal to the Court of Governors as Chairman of the Finance Committee, Barter made it clear that a decision to go ahead would definitely fall into the category made famous by the BBC's *Yes Minister* series of 'Very bold, Minister'. In Whitehall parlance such a warning meant anything from 'pretty risky' to 'positively unwise'. To avoid a project which might be a 'bridge too far', Barter advised governors to ask themselves: were they taking risks they should not be taking, what boundaries should be set on what could or could not be done, and how would the court keep the project within those boundaries to avoid the pitfalls of 'deal creep', where you keep going regardless of the consequences just because you have started? He added that he would only personally recommend it once he was 'absolutely convinced both as a property professional and as Chair of Finance there was a good enough prospect of it working'.

With the court fully informed, the key committees of estates, finance overseen by the Chairman's Committee, moved into action. This group examined what Stephen Barter called the 'viability triangle between "can we get the space that will work, can we get it commercially and can we do it safely?"' It helped that the space available was to be based in Thomas Cubitt's great landmark nineteenth-century Granary Warehouse with the former railway receiving sheds attached to the north. It helped that the architects for the work – part conversion, part development, part adaptation with a large dose of imagination – were Stanton Williams, responsible to UAL and accepted by the developers, Argent. It was essential that Argent agreed to take most of the construction risk onto their book. If Granary Square, as it became known, was to be the anchor for the whole of Argent's ambitious King's Cross development, it had to be a commercial success and an architectural landmark. Stanton Williams made sure it was.

Before Court decided to go ahead with a scheme far larger, far more ambitious, far costlier than Chelsea had been, it had to sell the two existing properties in Charing Cross Road and Southampton Row. Fortunately, UAL owned the freehold of both. Their disposal was an essential part of the financing of Granary Square; a large bank loan completed it. Once again, resistance from academic staff appeared. It took the form of lauding the essential contribution that the building itself had made to Saint Martins' record of creativity. Did the court not realize that decrepit premises were in truth the incubators of innovation? How could the University throw artists into a new, inevitably 'corporatized' development? The artist and governor Grayson Perry heard many such complaints of 'My God, it will be awful moving away from the centre of things, away from the "Bohemian Stonehenge that is Soho"!' There was, he said, 'a lot of sentimentality about creativity. A place becomes rundown.' (Charing Cross Road certainly was.) 'Artists like it.' (They did.) 'A lot of energy gathers there.' (It certainly had.) 'But how did you prevent it becoming a museum of the dirty parts of poverty?' (By creating a new, far better environment.)

Academic resistance to the departure from 'the Bohemian Stonehenge that was Soho' was overridden by three factors: the design of the building, the leadership of the college and the funding. Stanton Williams' design for the Cubitt Granary building was, despite academic fears, as 'uncorporate' as could be imagined. The walls in the teaching areas were lined with chipboard, openly described as 'sacrificial walls' to be used, marked, decorated, worked on or otherwise defaced as students wished, and finally to be cleaned and repainted at the year's end. A new college head was appointed, one fully committed to the ideas and potential of the new campus. And the supposed alternative of renovating the existing buildings would only provide an expensive, short-term, inadequate solution that UAL could not afford.

Grand vision as Granary Square was, the governors never succumbed to a fantasy image of what it might be. The sums involved were far too large for pretty dreaming. The three key committees, Estates, Finance and Chairman's, worked through the mass of detail, keeping, according to Lorraine Baldry, certain hard-nosed questions at the forefront of their minds: 'How would the building work? What would it cost? What did we have to forego? What would it look like? Could we afford it?' This thorough committee-based work informed discussions by the whole Court of Governors. There was no hiatus in the flow of information to the body ultimately responsible for the University's existence: governance was working soundly and properly.

One relationship was crucial in allowing the decision to build or not to build to be taken. As rector, Nigel Carrington saw the value in having a governor in Stephen Barter – a 'property man who knew property development backwards'. So close was their partnership that, 'I don't think Central Saint Martins would necessarily have happened, had there not been someone on Court who understood the dynamics of finishing negotiation on King's Cross in a way that allowed us reasonably confidently to proceed.'

Towards the end of 2008, decision time was imminent. It was a huge moment for all governors and for a rector only months into his post, who arrived with genuine doubts about whether to proceed. Barter finally advised that in his opinion while the 'financial viability was wafer-thin', it was there. We knew that 'Plan B' – to revamp the existing buildings – was a total non-starter. And there was always 'Plan C': Court could have 'done nothing'. As Carrington recalls, 'We could have frozen, there was an option, but it would have been a terrible mistake.' The decision to go ahead was not taken because there was no alternative. Court decided that the risks of a multi-million scheme were real and substantial, but they were as foreseeable and manageable as they could be. It helped to have as Chair of the Audit Committee a heavyweight 'Big Four' accountant, David Lindsell: 'Focussing on risk independently of the business is nuts. It's just the other side of opportunity. Be very clear about your risks but do so in conjunction with the opportunities.' Governors could sense the opportunities.

As we signed the documents to proceed with the Granary Square development on 3 November 2008, the financial world was literally collapsing all around us. We were not foolhardy; we signed knowing the governors had been clear-sighted about the risks, about the tightness of the financial margins, but to have walked away would have denied University of the Arts London the opportunity to take a landmark step forward. Court decided to seize the opportunity rather than back away from the risk. Every governor knew how big a decision faced them. As Stephen Barter recalled: 'We went round the room, one by one. Everyone had lived with it for six or seven years. How did we really feel about it now? It was very important to get everyone with the clearest understanding of what it was all about, the downsides, the upsides, all the risks. None of that was hidden.' The thoroughness of the decision-making and taking could not be overestimated. Cynical advice originally given to Carrington from University 'old hands' to 'avoid closeness with the Governors' had been shown to be desperately wrong. Cooperation and trust between governors and executives had made the historic project possible.

Four years later, on 18 September 2012, the University formally celebrated the opening of the 'Central Saint Martins campus in Granary Square'. It redefined the University, it reinforced the successful initiative provided by the Chelsea campus; it demonstrated that UAL was not a 'one-shot wonder'; it provided the hoped-for anchor for the development of the entire King's Cross site.

One question remained. However brilliant the campus might be, would its newness and unfamiliarity squeeze creativity out of the world-famous college? Grayson Perry, a frequent visitor, thinks not: 'It is the people who make the atmosphere, the culture. Sentimentality about the old place is dropping away. Culture is regenerating in the new building. International students like the grandeur.'

Unwittingly, events leading up to the opening of Granary Square threw a bright light onto what I still saw as a major weakness in UAL's standing. It had little sense of identity in the outside world and was still a loose confederation (at best) of six main colleges – Camberwell, Chelsea, Central Saint Martins, Wimbledon, London College of Fashion, London College of Communication. The University remained an administrative convenience to them, not a dynamic entity to which the colleges were inclined to cede identity. They lived in a world of 'exceptionalism' – that of their own uniqueness. How could they allow any derogation when they were so special? I persuaded Nigel Carrington and the court that a coherent university identity would benefit colleges, not diminish them. I saw it as a 'zero-plus' game from which all would gain; colleges insisted on regarding any increase in university identity as a 'zero-sum' game, one where everyone lost. It was after all the University in practice that was shaping, enabling and guaranteeing the future existence and prosperity of the colleges. It could not be brushed aside as a mere convenience. Besides, unifying university identity was not a piece of image-making, it also indicated that colleges were wasting money by sticking to their old administrative ways as if true identity depended on mere difference.

Before the formal opening of the campus we decided to have a 'soft' opening the previous academic year. To my astonishment, the draft invitation came from the Head of College rather than from the chairman, rector and University. This indicated a total failure to understand that without the University and the Court of Governors, Central Saint Martins at Granary Square, King's Cross would not exist. How could the College imagine that they could lay claim to the project regardless of the reality of how it had been created? It demonstrated how weak was any idea of university, how entrenched were old 'college-first' attitudes, how much needed to be done to shift old ways of thinking and behaving.

In the following months, Nigel Carrington and I had a tug of war over the speed with which we pressed for a stronger, clearer, more coherent idea of the University. I wanted a new visual identity and logo which put the University first and embraced the colleges clearly within that identity. Both, I believed, would be strengthened as a result. Nigel and I agreed that the University identity should and could be built up without harming the separate heritage of the colleges. We disagreed over the speed at which it could be done. He approached it from his experience of introducing similar changes at his law firm: 'If I just put a proposition to the executive board, it wouldn't work. In fact, every year we made steady steps to bring the University into more consistency. They are incremental ultimately with people's consent, if not enthusiastic approval. I completely agreed with you, I just didn't think I could do it faster. I had to spend time with people, I had to pick them off, one by one.'

We never fell out over the matter of speed. I never doubted that Nigel would act. An impatient chair, a considered rector; perhaps my impatience, or urgency, helped rather than hindered him. For the Secretary and Registrar, Steven Marshall, with a close-up view of the relationship, it came close to a definition of good governance: 'The role of the Chair is to push and provoke. The role of the Vice-Chancellor is to respond. It's "push-pull", that is what happened.'

Nigel Carrington and I worked together closely for five years. I liked him as a human being, admired him as a leader and professional manager. We never fell out and where we disagreed, did so without rancour. Our mutual trust was total and never violated. It took a fellow governor, Lorraine Baldry, to put her finger on what made our relationship work. I was a journalist, she observed, he a lawyer: 'You couldn't be more different and that made you very complementary. The issue for you was news, of the moment. If you didn't do something, it was a missed opportunity whereas for Nigel, it wasn't a question of missing an opportunity, you had to go through a process.' Such different approaches proved useful and constructive: Nigel's caution would temper my urgency, my wish for speed would shape his tactics. Crucially, governors and executives saw no conflict in our shared sense of purpose for UAL or in our determination to pursue a united sense of direction. But it should never have been taken for granted, according to Carrington: 'We could legitimately have had different views. That is where in any organization you actually have to part company. Either the Chair has to go or the Chief Exec has to go. If they can't operate together, the organization isn't going to thrive.' That situation never arose or came close to arising in our five years together.

Not everyone took us at our own estimation. Some staff regarded Nigel as a mere 'property developer', others judged me to be dogmatic centralizer. Both were wide of the mark.

Between becoming a university in 2004 and my departure from the Chair of the Governing Body in 2013, University of the Arts London transformed itself. Two major unified college campuses were built; a clearer university identity was created without taking away from the individual strengths and character of the colleges; the Court of Governors was strong without ever trespassing on executive or academic matters; the vice-chancellor worked closely with governors and proved how right we had been to appoint him.

None of this would have been achieved without strong governance. Had external supervision not been set up from the moment of the banding together of the five colleges of the London Institute in 1988, they would have pursued their separate ways along the road to oblivion or irrelevance. Governance created a sense of purpose, a desire for achievement, a belief in potential, a method of delivery. It was not an obstruction, still less an imposition. Indeed, it was the essential condition for the success of University of the Arts London.

One appointment above all demonstrated that Nigel Carrington and I had the feel and spirit of UAL right. The exuberant ceramicist Grayson Perry became Chancellor of the University in 2015, a titular role most important for presiding over degree day ceremonies, those heart-warming gatherings of achievement, fulfilment and togetherness. This he did in the outrageously costumed, full transvestite figure of his alter-ego Claire.

He looked splendid. So, what was his role on these occasions? 'I was a kind of spiritual figurehead, an exemplar that embodies the spirit of the institution, creativity, inventiveness. I was the ambassador for the messy workings of the institution rather than an apparatchik of the institution.' Could a university of the arts, for the arts, about the arts, ask for more?

REFLECTIONS

Creating a governing body for an academic institution is essential for progress.

The governing body should be the forum for the external governors. It should not be overweighted with academic officials and representatives.

If meetings of the governing body are dominated by academics, why should 'lay' members give their time and attention to it?

The quantity and detail of papers set before the governing body should facilitate effective supervision. Sheer volume of papers should not be used to obstruct and frustrate. Too much information is almost worse than too little.

Knowledge of the University is better spread by contacts outside and beyond formal meetings of the governing body. Insisting on membership of the body is to fetishize it.

Managers who evade governor scrutiny do not understand the nature of university governance.

The Chair of the Governing Body and the Vice-Chancellor may be different in temperament but must be united in a vision for the University. There are different ways of implementing an agreed vision.

There is a useful 'push-pull' element in the chair/vice-chancellor relationship. It may not matter who does what, but both 'pushing forward' and 'pulling back' are needed for good balance.

The wise vice-chancellor will not feel threatened by the skills and expertise of members of the governing body but will harness them to the University's needs.

An active and engaged chair is not an interfering one.

Without a vision, a university will lack purpose and direction.

The default option for many academics is to suggest delay – an avoidance mechanism which avoids decisions and only costs money. The default option for trades unions in an academic environment is almost always to seek delay without considering the costs incurred.

Delay is delay; it is worse than postponing a decision.

Too many staff and union members of a governing body find it hard to consider the best interests of the University rather than the special interests of those they may feel they represent. Staff and union members who think and act in this way are far less useful as members of the governing body.

Often academics are not reliable judges of a university's best interests or future direction. To the extent that they speak up for their own interests, they are invalidated from acting as disinterested supervisors.

Compiling 'risk registers' can become an obsession and a substitute for actual management of risks. Merely identifying and listing risks does not make an organization actively risk aware.

Most risk registers are too long. Are they balanced by a matching 'Opportunity Register?' Should they not be?

Concentrating on risks creates a negative cast of mind while focussing on opportunities can transform the process of taking decisions.

Having a vision of the opportunities provided by property deals allowed the governors to transform University of the Arts London, academically and creatively. Academics did not contribute to the vision or its realization.

The most involved governors were the most useful governors.

The days of the 'four-meetings-and-an-away-day' per year governor are over.

'Lay' governors do not 'know best', they may 'know different'.

Academics and artists can get very sentimental about the sources and sites of creativity.

A governing body will have business and similar skills represented on it. This does not make it a 'pseudo-company' board.

A governing board will examine the business effectiveness of the University. If they don't, who will? No UAL governor from a business or professional background ever confused the University with a business.

If a conflict of interest arises, it is better to face up to it at an early stage.

Just because governors ask questions about teaching does not mean they know the answers or want to interfere.

University governors give their time freely and willingly without financial reward. They are unpaid volunteers. If the cost of their time was measured, it would be very large.

This commitment should never be taken for granted or undervalued, but acknowledged and recognized. Civil society is enriched by such generosity of spirit.

7

Clore Leadership Programme (CLP): Shaping an Idea – Governance in a 'Start-up' (2008–2014)

Interviews with

Farooq Chaudhry, Trustee, 2004–12; Executive Producer, Akram Khan Company (AKC)

Sue Hoyle, Clore Leadership Programme, 2003–17, Deputy Director, 2003–08, Director, 2008–17

David Kershaw, Trustee; CEO, M&C Saatchi

Nichola Johnson, Chair, Clore Leadership Programme, 2004–08

Prue Skene, governance consultant; Chair, Cardboard Citizens

Lord Smith of Finsbury, Director, Clore Leadership Programme, 2003–08

In September 2008, I had a phone call from the headhunter Liz Amos. The Clore Leadership Programme (CLP), brainchild of the powerful arts philanthropist, Dame Vivien Duffield, was looking for an executive chairman to lead the programme on the departure of its founding director, Chris Smith (Lord Smith of Finsbury). It would involve working closely with the new director, Sue Hoyle. As a part-time paid position, it required two days a week as well as attendance at some residential courses at the heart of the programme. So, I thought about it long and hard. I knew the work of the CLP over its first five years, strongly admired its aim of creating the next generation of arts leaders. At the Barbican we had had a succession of Clore Fellows on secondment as part of their fellowship programme. In addition, I had mentored at least three of them. The CLP – later re-named 'Clore Fellowship' – was original, ambitious, special, clearly focussed and almost certainly unique in the often-woolly worlds of arts leadership training.

I looked closely at the demands on my time. Two days a week seemed hardly enough for the wide range of duties and responsibilities expected of an executive chairman; it would almost certainly be more. But it was manageable and fitted well with my existing commitments at University of the Arts London (UAL). Two aspects stirred my curiosity in particular: unlike the other boards in which I had been involved, this was very young, in effect a 'start-up'. How would governance work when you were starting from scratch? More interesting still was the presence on the trustee board of the founder and principal funder of the CLP, Dame Vivien Duffield. This was a 'funder-led' start-up. How would she use her influence? Could that lead to a conflict of interest? How independently could trustees act with such an overwhelming presence in their midst? I decided that it would be worth finding out and told Liz Amos I would apply.

When news of my application became public, several people tried to warn me off, some fairly vehemently. Dame Vivien, a figure as powerful as she was controversial in the arts world, was usually at the heart of their warnings. They were less about the potential problems for governance raised by the presence of the prime mover on the trustee board, more about perceived judgements about Dame Vivien's style and character. I noted the warnings, had my own view and was pleased to be called for interview on 22 October 2008. It was over very quickly. The interview was conducted by a high-powered group including Dame Vivien herself and Sir Nicholas Serota, Director of Tate. Liz Amos rang within a few hours and asked if I would accept the appointment. I had no hesitation in saying that I would. Clearly, the Clore Fellowship board could make up its mind quickly and decisively.

It had done so from its very beginnings at the start of the 2000s. Dame Vivien was a member of many of the influential arts boards in London and often a member of the appointment boards to the leadership of these institutions. She was increasingly dismayed to find, as she often put it, the same old faces and people turning up at board after board, many of whom she had previously rejected. As she once said directly to Nicholas Serota, 'I'm fed up with old white men like you running these things.' She would tell the grand panjandrums of the arts world to their faces and in public that she wanted them replaced by new and younger blood. The talent pool for top-level leadership was, in her view, drained dry; the nation's institutions needed better leadership, and quickly.

In 2002, the Clore Duffield Foundation commissioned two leading arts consultants, John Holden and Robert Hewison, to draw up a scheme for a leadership development programme. Reporting in December 2002, they defined leadership as 'the ability to conceive and articulate a direction and purpose and to work with others to achieve that purpose in both benign and hostile circumstances'. It judged the time was ripe for a 'constructive intervention' in leadership, examining how leaders would 'adapt and modify themselves in the light of experience'.

Holden/Hewison set out a programme to assist this process. Over a period of two years up to 25 'Clore Fellows' would develop as future leaders through a programme of residential courses, secondments and mentoring. The courses would enable and encourage self-examination and self-discovery. Secondments would be to organizations quite different from the fellow's own discipline, while the mentoring would assist in developing self-awareness. The result would not lead to a formal qualification; there would be no course modules; it would not be a 'taught' fellowship but a 'learned' one based on acquiring personal experience of and about themselves and how they might lead. Perhaps most importantly, Holden/Hewison insisted cultural organizations were 'values-based enterprises – the issue was not simply "value for money" but "money for values"'. Commendably succinct, it was directed to a purpose. Fifteen years on, it is easy to underestimate its radical nature. If Holden/Hewison read Dame Vivien's mind accurately, they also built a structure that turned her initial impulse into reality.

Within six months, by July 2003, the executive team was appointed; the former politician and Culture Secretary, Lord Smith of Finsbury, Chris Smith, became the first director, working part-time; Sue Hoyle, with years of experience at the Arts Council and leadership roles in dance, joined as full-time deputy director. In a little over a year, the entire Clore Fellowship Programme had been devised in detail, the first cohort of fellows recruited to start in September 2004. For a 'start-up' to move from the first thought to the beginning of activity within two years was incredibly fast. Might this set an example that others could follow? Chris Smith thinks it was replicable on certain simple-sounding conditions: 'Number one, make sure your idea is good!' (Holden/Hewison tested it.) 'Number two, make the shape of the idea reasonably clear so that you can invite people to join the board'. (Holden/Hewison put flesh on the skeleton outline.) 'Number three, find board members who are committed to the idea, really believe in what the organization is doing, and who are not there simply because they fancy being on a board'. (They did.) If governance appeared to come third in the process, it was not that it did not matter, just that the substance of the project had to come first. How it should be governed would evolve as the project took shape.

Dame Vivien now did this in her own inimitable manner. This was a start-up – *her* start-up, *her* money. She would not be the chairman, that was never her style. Nor was this the time for the formal processes of board appointment through a nominations committee. (There wasn't one.) In the words of one of the founding board members, Nichola Johnson, 'Vivien brought on "rabbit's friends and relations"' – an affectionate reference to A.A. Milne's *The House at Pooh Corner*. They were some of the closest, most trusted contacts of her existing cultural family – Sir Nicholas Serota, Director of Tate, Lord Hall, Chief Executive of the Royal Opera, Sir Nicholas Hytner, Director of the National Theatre. Nobody else could have assembled such a heavyweight board of powerhouse trustees in this way at such speed, if at all. It demonstrated several things: that the Clore Leadership Programme initiative was serious and was to be taken seriously. Dame Vivien was personally committed to it. And these board supporters met her need for people who she liked, who were established in their position and who would also stand up to her. For David Kershaw, an old friend, 'This was a very brave punt for her and she wanted people who she knew and trusted.' Combative as she was, often described as a 'force of nature', Dame Vivien also wanted challenge. Any detached observer would have recognized it as a 'brilliant board'.

All those on it knew that the needs of a 'funder-led start-up' were totally different from those of a well-established organization. According to Nichola Johnson, the second chairman, board discussions were structured but above all informal. This became the key aspect of a gathering which started in advisory mode and morphed into more organized form as the Fellowship developed. Farooq Chaudhry, Executive Director of Akram Khan Company (AKC), is clear about that: 'It felt more intuitive, conversational. Creative as well as looking rigorously at finance. It was more porous, about relationships in the room, less defined. It always felt a group of individuals with expertise but not just about expertise. The way they looked at the world made it different from other boards I knew.'

As a result, Chaudhry felt that people were less inhibited, which had a real effect on the discussions: 'Responsibility is a funny thing. It comes with a sense of expectation, a burden almost, that you will contribute something organized.' He described it as an almost parental response of responsibility. Whereas when you are 'with friends, the discussion is more free-flowing, you are not so worried about what the minutes will say, it is less inhibited'.

For David Kershaw, founder partner of M&C Saatchi and a long-standing colleague of Dame Vivien, the board atmosphere was 'informal but full of the excitement of a new organization.' Filled with strong personalities and interesting thoughts, they felt able to 'think more about the issues of what we were doing than a lot of other boards I sat on. In terms of intellectual output and willingness to look at change, it was productive, a terrific board to sit on.' He adds that it was good for those involved too: 'It's nice to spend time with clever people, it is good for your soul and you tend to come up with better thinking because you have the collective thinking of interesting minds.'

There is no evidence that this gathering of the 'great and good' of the arts world led to displays of egotism, of competitive clashes of personality. Perhaps because it was a start-up, perhaps because imagination and innovation were called for, perhaps because the governance was itself being developed, the board atmosphere had a precious quality of togetherness that other boards would envy and should learn from. Perhaps it was just very grown-up.

There was a further, unexpected ingredient involved, according to Farooq Chaudhry: 'Hard work can be fun, can be playful. I use the analogy with the creative process. Sometimes you source ideas in a more free-flowing way. It allows things to turn around, to meander until they find themselves. Even though there was an agenda, we could have very free-flowing conversations.' The notion of a 'meander' as a route to creative decision-making is as attractive as it is unorthodox. Yet viewed from the outside by a long-standing governance consultant and board chair, Prue Skene, 'The Clore set up was never terribly clear. It didn't seem like a normal board of trustees.' (It wasn't.) 'Nobody seemed to be able to answer the question of what was the governance structure.' Which did not stop it from being effective.

The new executive team of Chris Smith, Director, and Sue Hoyle, Deputy Director, had months, not years to turn the Holden/Hewison blueprint into a working fellowship programme. This might have tested relations between executives and the board had there not been a shared vision and mutual trust. Smith recalls that the demarcation of responsibilities was always clearly understood. Hoyle describes it thus: 'Chris and I would work up a proposal on part of the programme, then go to the board to test our thinking and get approval. Typically, we were getting sign-off and advice from them on all the things that we needed to put in place to launch the programme.' More informally, Smith recalls, 'We were making it up as we went along.' They all were; one key part of governance was running smoothly.

At the same time, another element was being tested: relations between the chair and chief executive over which so many organizations come to grief to this day. Chris Smith had had a long career in politics: he would not be a deferential kind of executive, not easily biddable, rather the opposite. The first Chair of the Clore Leadership Programme, Sir Clive Gillinson, Chief Executive of the London Symphony Orchestra (LSO), soon left to run the Carnegie Center in New York. A new chair was needed. Nichola Johnson had created and run a highly successful leadership course for museum directors at the University of East Anglia and was already on the CLP board. According to her recollection: 'When Clive left for New York, there was no formal interview for the Chair; there were no terms of reference for the post. Vivien effectively just said to me, "You do it." I had nothing to lose by taking it.' If the selection process was informal, the result was effective.

How would Johnson and Smith hit it off? He defined the chair/CEO relationship as one founded in good mutual chemistry. Beyond that: 'The Chair had to be prepared to let the Director run with things, having made a judgement as to whether this was likely to be a complete disaster or not. But the Chair must not be someone who interfered all the time. They must be prepared to stand back and let things happen even if it wasn't necessarily the Chair's idea in the first place.' That could be described as a very strong establishment of a 'forward' definition of executive primacy. Nichola Johnson merely observes, 'Chris Smith was always in control of the organization.' Another board member cautioned: 'Chris was very powerful. He was hard to control, a real heavyweight.' There is no reason to doubt Smith's own recollection that 'We were all finding our way and that is what made it so exciting.' They were all driven by an overriding sense of purpose; the nuances of power relationships came second.

Evidence exists for only one disagreement between chair and director in this period. It was over a review of the programme after its first five years. In hindsight, Sue Hoyle regrets that a review was not built into the programme from the outset to judge impact and how it should be measured. According to Nichola Johnson, Chris Smith found it hard to accept and seemed to become rather defensive about such scrutiny. Given the CLP's clear success and professional approval, this seems strange. One explanation might be that while the arts world is thick with appraisal and external assessment, the Whitehall and Westminster world is characterized by scrutiny and challenge that are open to rejection or rebuttal. These are very different processes. The director was brought up in the latter environment, was much less comfortable with the former. It was a culture clash. At all events, the final review delivered general approval with suggestions for improvement. It was hardly a crisis of governance.

In this 'start-up', the director also had to keep the confidence of its progenitor and funder, Dame Vivien Duffield. Chris Smith is clear: 'During the whole five years that I was Director, she believed in what we were doing, she thought we were doing it well, and she let us run with it. There was no sense at any point that she was disappointed, that it wasn't delivering what she had expected it to deliver, that we weren't performing as she had hoped we would.'

The only possible area of concern might have been over timing: when would the CLP have started to visibly transform the arts leadership landscape? When would the new generation get the 'Nick Serotas, the Tony Halls and Nick Hytners' – as she loved putting it – to move over from centre stage? From the outset, recalls Nichola Johnson, with years of personal experience of developing museum leaders, 'We warned Vivien, "This is a slow burn, it could take 10 years". If Dame Vivien ever felt frustrated, she did not show it. She took the long view and trusted her chosen executive team.

Such were the ingredients of one particular and successful funder-led start-up. A good idea, a strong backer, available and assured funding, clear blueprint, powerful informally gathered board, carefully chosen executive, good partnership between them, shared vision, coherent implementation ... just nine key ingredients driven by practicality, not dogma. It might be argued that only the first and the last mattered – the original good idea, the coherent implementation. Yet the intermediate ingredients were essential too and all were guided by an approach to governance which evolved from the informal and inspirational to the organized and systematic. The result was that after just four years in existence, the Clore Leadership Programme was recognized as unique in the field of leadership development.

When Chris Smith decided to stand down after five years, the board had a major decision to take about organization. The existing leadership structure was perfectly conventional: a strong executive working to a supervising chair and board. Nichola Johnson saw at once, 'We needed a different board structure after Chris.' They looked for a 'high-profile public chair' to maintain the CLP's public presence. While Sue Hoyle had proved a brilliant deputy director, how would she fare in the far more exposed role as director? Collectively, the board took the decision to switch the public presence role of the CLP from the director to a part-time executive chairman. Hence the job description presented to me. At interview, they raised at least two questions: could I restrain my strong executive instincts to become a 'part-time executive chair'? Would this new balance at the top allow Sue Hoyle to move up from the deputy role to actual leadership with full executive responsibility? I had no doubts about my answer to either question.

This was the situation when I became part-time executive chairman in 2008. While never anxious about my relationship with Dame Vivien, I understood that if I lost her confidence, I would not last long. I had no problem with that. While other funders such as Arts Council England had rapidly joined in, while the sense of an understood purpose was extremely strong among board, executive and administrators, the whole project had 'Vivien Duffield' strongly stamped over it. This had never been glossed over or ignored in governance terms. The charity world contains many individuals whose personality is closely identified with a particular cause. In charity law any such individual must be clearly recognized and identified as a 'Person of Significant Control' (PSC). Some might say that the label was inadequate to capture the full extent of Dame Vivien's influence over Clore Leadership in practice. Of course, the reality of 'control' existed in the fact that had the Clore Duffield Foundation withdrawn funding, the Fellowship could not have continued. That sounds like control in any language. Dame Vivien never opposed a range of sometimes radical changes to the detailed design of the fellowships that constituted Sue Hoyle's 'quiet revolution'. Since they were consistent with the CLP's founding purposes, they required scrutiny, but if they passed muster would face no kind of obstruction. Personally, Dame Vivien was solicitous, asking Sue and me: 'Are you alright? Are you happy with what you are doing? Is there anything I can do for you?' She meant it. Her support was never in doubt and massively reassuring.

She became most vocal over the actual choice of the 25 Clore Fellows each year. The process of reducing a shortlist of 80 applicants to two dozen fellows involved several weeks of hour-long interviews. Dame Vivien often joined in an entire day, an essential way of keeping in touch with the approach to selection and the practical considerations driving it. The convention then was that once a candidate had left the interview room, no panel member would state an opinion before everyone had analyzed that candidate's performance in detail. Fair process demanded such discipline. But with Dame Vivien present, on occasion the door had barely swung shut on a candidate before she declared, 'Well, they're not right, are they?' The truth was she was almost always correct in her judgement. Disruptive or stimulating? At least it bound her into the process.

More questioning emerged at arguably the key day in the Clore Fellowship year – the final selection of fellows at a full board meeting. Dame Vivien always had her eye on the prize, albeit a distant one: the possible successor to the 'Serotas, Halls, Hytners', etc. She understood that in the nature of things, not every fellow would meet the highest standards of future excellence and authority she was seeking. Most would contribute, shape and perhaps transform arts organizations of many kinds and sizes in small or specific ways. She was a realist and besides, such a range of impact across the arts scene was always an understood part of the CLP agenda. But Dame Vivien would question the suitability of candidates she judged to be too old and past their ability to develop or what she believed were not art forms at all, such as street theatre and circus performers. Her special wrath was reserved for what she once described to me as 'mucked-up art forms', meaning most kinds of 'cross arts activity'. Sometimes she gave way, accepting our arguments but having made her points. On occasion, we beat a tactical retreat over a particular individual in anticipation of major disagreement. The number of really disputed candidates over seven years was small. I never regarded it as coming close to 'throwing her weight around', to abuse of her position of 'significant control'. It was a valuable part of the cut and thrust of assessment and debate. Yet the challenge of having a person of such influence on the board – the first funder, principal founder and assured, continuing funder – should not be underestimated. Director Sue Hoyle was in many respects closer to the subtlety of the problems it raised: 'She liked to be involved in decision-making. What were the decisions you could take without her involvement and where were the decisions that you needed to consult on? She asked questions that were incredibly unexpected and usually very pertinent.'

For a board member such as Farooq Chaudhry it was very unusual to have the 'owner of the project' on the board. And yet: 'She was the perfect example of someone who could cut through the issues to get down to the human "nitty-gritty", to think you might be uncomfortable talking about. She is a person who makes things happen.' But there were also reservations: 'It felt hard to challenge. You had to be careful, "the boss is in the room".'

One of Dame Vivien's closest friends and long-standing colleagues, David Kershaw, observes evenly: 'Vivien does not tend to have neutral views. She says what she thinks and really believes and whoever it upsets, tough. If you're the funder, you can do that in a more robust way than if you were just another member of the Board. There's no point in pretending that she can't and doesn't behave differently.'

The fact is that any such interventions did not divert the CLP executives from doing what Dame Vivien and the board had set out to do. She herself was powerfully reinforced in her support for the scheme by the fact that wherever she went in the arts world, somebody would introduce themselves as a 'Clore Fellow' and thank her for transforming their life.

By now, the board and board systems had become more orthodox, dealing with business in properly conventional ways without wholly losing the brio and exhilaration of the start-up years. Sue Hoyle recalls them as 'Enjoyable, efficient, practical' and (a key indicator), 'I could ask board members for advice outside the meeting, which was really important.'

I recall in particular two areas of weakness: one a failure and the other an oddity.

The oddity was that the Clore Fellowship did not address governance full-on as a topic in the early years. There were occasional sessions on the subject at awaydays but it was not built into the core of the learning programme. For some, it was hard to fit in at the outset. The subject was parked, it was not seen as a number one priority. Chris Smith confirms governance was left out as a key ingredient because 'ultimately, we realized that we couldn't cover absolutely everything. We were trying to cover the most important and difficult things.' The passing of time also comes into it, as Nichola Johnson observed: 'Fifteen years ago, governance was not on the agenda as an item in the way it is today. On reflection, it's odd that it was left out since as future leaders Fellows would be at the receiving end of governance.' Adding, 'Perhaps they were too young to need it yet.' My own view is that the subject was rightly felt to be too difficult and understandable only after considerable experience of good and bad governance in practice. Most fellows were too young to have the necessary background experience. Even if the practicalities of board business could be described, we all knew that the human complexities of board interactions were not easily rendered into chunks of learning – they had to be experienced personally first. While governance was a topic that we nagged away at in various forms over time, I never felt it to be at the heart of the Clore experience.

If that was the oddity, the failure not to innovate at the 10-year point was more revealing. Precisely because Sue Hoyle and I were confident that the CLP was doing what it set out to do, we commissioned a review into barriers to leadership development and suggested a broad examination of aims, results, effects and omissions. Or in management-speak, 'Objectives, intentions, outcomes, impacts, deliverables, risks and negatives'. It might take time, might be a diversion of effort and would certainly cost money. On balance, we feared complacency was more of a danger after a decade of achievement.

When we presented our proposals to the board, Dame Vivien produced one of her hand grenades. Why was all this needed? 'We don't need all this Jewish angst!' I observed that it might also be an excess of 'Protestant conscience'. This was a major board intervention. Their sense was that digging up the programme by the roots or at least probing very deeply was unnecessary. A 'light touch' review might help and who better to do it than the authors of the original defining report, John Holden and Robert Hewison? In truth, they were never going to redesign their own scheme root and branch. In due course, their 'light touch' review proved to be just that: respectable, reassuring but not radical.

The board's reluctance to approve a radical review was neither an excess of governance nor a failure but a proper exercise of their strategic responsibility. There was a view later that the review was too 'light touch'. Some judged the Clore Fellowship as weak on data collection and impact assessment and looked for more rigorous self-questioning on the lines of 'Why do we exist? What have we done? What will we do?' In practice,

Sue Hoyle subtly but significantly reshaped elements of the Fellowship Programme every year. Pragmatic adjustments guided by a clear sense of purpose, they may not have been driven by probing, fundamental challenges but they did demonstrate a lot of critical self-awareness.

My sense of failure over this was personal. I liked the 'light touch' approach. Its reassuring conclusions suited me and endorsed the kind of contributions that I felt I made in the Fellowship Programme. The atmosphere on the courses and sessions was rich, warm, inclusive and perhaps too comfortable. I had worked within that environment fruitfully and was reluctant to imagine a totally different one. Major change would not come from me as executive chairman. Soon it would be time to move on but it raised doubts about my own capacity to manage change.

Farooq Chaudhry has faced this challenge in his own career: 'The hardest thing is to renew when you are successful. How do you re-imagine an organization? It is almost as if you have to deliberately shut it down and reinvent it. Think of it as a "project" rather than as a fixed entity. A "project" has by definition to come to an end. It gives you time to breathe and reflect and then come back.' Not only is this a bracing way to approach change, it identifies an important piece of psychology: 'We like institutions! It is reassuring to board members. It causes anxiety when you say the time has come to renew a project.'

In his world, David Kershaw believes in a state of constant questioning and challenging, a kind of 'Maoist permanent revolution' of thinking. He recognizes the situation where a chair or chief executive arrives and asks the huge questions in the first six months: 'The real issue is, are you capable of the next revolution? That is why boards and chairs need to be refreshed to get new thinking in.' Perhaps my own response reflected difficulty in thinking of Clore Fellowship as a 'project', being too comfortable in it as a nascent 'institution' and being unable to move beyond my own first satisfying experiences of it.

There were lessons about governance to be learned for all, board members and fellows alike. Every member of the CLP board had years of experience of governance in all shapes and sizes. Had they been asked to pass on their lessons, they might have included some of these observations.

Farooq Chaudhry from Akram Khan Company explained why they chose a different chair every four or five years in relation to the company's state of development and current needs. The first chair balanced financial discipline while encouraging ambition and risk; the second was appointed to 'tidy up the machinery' of the company; the third addressed internal conflicts of opinion and leadership psychology. A priority for the fourth chair might be to develop the company's entrepreneurial skills. At each stage, AKC looked for a mindset that addressed the challenges the company was facing. AKC has always taken its time in choosing its governance. Farooq's practical watchword: 'We take as much care in choosing a board member as a dancer!' Crucially, each chair has understood they were involved in a dance company, not a business.

From chairing major public organizations, Chris Smith's advice was distilled down to three essentials. If they sound simple in the way he states them, they are harder to put into practice: 'The importance of choosing the right person to run the organization. The importance of every single member of the board being passionate about what the organization is about. The importance of knowing where that boundary between supervision and interference actually lies.'

When Prue Skene advises on governance, she devotes time to this dividing line. She is clear in her own mind exactly where it lies: 'Management (the executive) is where the ideas, discussion and strategy are drafted and formed. These are the people who work in the organization 365 days in the year. Then it comes to the Board for development and ultimate approval. It's not a difficult balance and it should be a helpful one. I've heard it said that boards are responsible for initiating strategy. Absolutely not, they're not!'

Sue Hoyle saw many troubled arts boards at work before she joined CLP. Such disagreement was never an edifying sight, internal strife had a bad effect on any organization: 'When a board doesn't work, nothing happens. They're incapable of taking decisions, of handling the necessary risks involved in an arts organization. When boards are so troubled they spend all their time fighting one another rather than getting on with business, it can be really damaging for an organization because it loses momentum, a sense of purpose and it becomes impossible to take decisions.' In her view, the chair has full responsibility for the way the board acts and behaves, but the executive must provide a full flow of information to the board. Good governance is always a shared responsibility.

With years of experience on commercial, charity and arts boards, David Kershaw now finds himself deeply concerned about the volume of material boards have to address over compliance, responsibility and risk aversion, what he calls 'a creeping disease, an avalanche of crap'. It drives out strategic thinking and obliges boards to find time outside normal business to think, speculate and do all the things they should do and that he could do in the early days of the CLP. Boards may not formulate strategy but they have a bigger role than becoming an organ for ratifying box ticking, which gives pride of place to compliance and the exercise of accountability.

Had Kershaw been asked directly, he would have reassured Clore Fellows about the complexity of the arts world they lived and worked in. In the commercial world, good quality must be delivered and shareholders judge. The arts world, he insists, is far more complex: 'How do you judge the quality of what you produce? How do you measure that? By audience numbers? By critical acclaim? At the same time there is an objective not to lose money. Balancing the output which is hard to measure versus the financial risk is very complex. The wiring is more dense.' Does this complexity in the activity of the arts affect the complexity of sitting on an arts board? He is emphatic: 'I would slap people down if they ever said that arts boards are easy!'

The Clore Fellowship was a case study in the governance of a 'funder-led start-up' project. It began in an atmosphere of inspiration and informality that produced a liberating spirit, which freed inhibition among the board. It evolved into a more formal board which never wholly lost the exhilaration of its early years. On its board it accommodated the powerful person who began it, was the first funder and continued funding. It contained some of the most powerful figures in the national arts scene, who left their egos at the door. The board appointed leaders who combined effectively, trusted its appointed executives to do their job and took decisions at the right strategic level.

The Clore Fellowship guided half a generation of arts leaders into greater understanding of their own abilities, advanced their leadership skills, provided them with practical skills they might have lacked and equipped them with a good dose of critical self-knowledge. Within 15 years of its inception, it had achieved one of its original goals: Clore Fellows were filling some of the biggest posts in the national arts world. From 'start-up' to success, from a good idea to actual results in 15 years is extremely rapid.

REFLECTIONS

When creating an organization from scratch, test the idea to make sure it is good. A good idea needs to be supported by a sound framework.

People will only join a new board if it has clear ideas backed by a good organization.

A 'start-up' board cannot be created through the formal processes of a nominations committee. It will usually consist of friends and personal contacts. There is nothing wrong with this. In such circumstances, the personal is the professional.

In the early years of a 'start-up', governance can be light. As the project grows, governance will develop in line with its needs. In those early years, board discussion should be uninhibited, exploratory and fun.

Good governance knows the rules by which it should behave but also the spirit in which it behaves.

A 'Person of Significant Control' on a board will know the limits of their influence.

Time spent in identifying board chairs and board members can never be wasted.

Boards that give time to ideas are more useful than boards that spend time ticking boxes. Compliance is important, but innovation is essential.

Board discussions should find time to be free-flowing. A good 'meander' can lead to a creative result.

Do not remain on a board that devotes more time to the accountable rather than the speculative. It is possible to speculate without interfering with the executive.

Boards cannot primarily develop strategy, that is the task of the executive. The executive proposes, but the board disposes.

A board at war with itself damages the whole organization. Internecine warfare on a board is an indulgence and a diversion of proper effort.

A successful organization can fall in love with its own success; that is the time to try fresh thinking. Are you capable of the 'next revolution'?

Any 'start-up' should consider whether it is really a 'project' with a limited lifespan or truly a long-term institution.

Shutting down a successful 'project' may be the necessary condition for fresh innovation.

People love institutions; we are reassured by them. It feels threatening when their existence is questioned.

Radical self-questioning is not the only way to keep things fresh. Regular improvement can be just as effective.

Arts boards are complex and difficult by their nature. Ignore anyone who thinks they are not.

Arts organizations and their boards should stop having an inferiority complex about their commercial counterparts.

8

Reflecting on Reflections

Anyone joining a board is deluged with manuals, rules, regulations, warnings and consequences. The first three tell of your fiduciary duties as a board member, what you must do by law. The next warns of the results – usually unpleasant – if you fall down in your duties. The last threatens you with consequences ranging from personal financial liability for debts incurred to a ban from ever sitting on a board again. All three – regulations, warnings, consequences – are real and important. Yet observing all of them will not make an effective board or the diligent individual a good board member. No amount of codification, regulation or prescription has ever caught – or attempted to catch – the single essential element for good board practice and behaviour: the human factor. Good governance depends on good behaviour. No one has ever found a way of defining how individuals should behave on a board. Too many behave badly. Governance sounds legalistic and bureaucratic. In fact, it is an entirely human activity. Why does it appear to be so difficult to behave properly in the governance environment? Why do chairs and chief executives not get on? Why do boards appoint the wrong chairs and chief executives? Why do so many board members have the wrong expectations about what they can do, how they should act? There is no definitive answer to these questions. Perhaps some of my experiences can shed light on them.

The quality of chairmen I have served under covers the spectrum from the really good to the truly awful. At the Barbican Centre, a very senior City leader and lawyer, Michael Cassidy, understood exactly what I, as Managing Director, and Graham Sheffield, as Arts Director, were trying to do: to release the Barbican's potential and turn it into a major international arts centre. He also knew how to shape, steer and modify our ambitions through the processes of the City of London Corporation, our principal funder. When Cassidy advised caution or delay, it was not obstruction but canny tactics. A master of the art of the possible in a local authority, no matter how rich it was, he controlled my impatience, tempered our enthusiasms with his deep understanding of political practicalities. There was never a moment of doubt about the shared nature of our ambition and sense of direction for the Barbican. For me as Chief Executive, Michael Cassidy was the ideal chairman.

As a board member, I served under three exemplary chairs. In the United States on the board of Public Radio International (PRI) in Minneapolis, Kenneth Dayton presided with decency, humanity and rigour. As wise as he was generous, he and his wife Judy Dayton were exemplary in their insistence that it was the duty of the rich to give. Dayton codified his thoughts on giving and governance and these texts became foundation pieces for the US philanthropic sector. He scrutinized his chief executives and expected to be scrutinized in his turn. There was no personal vanity in him; his authority, benign and strong, sprang from modesty.

In the United Kingdom, Niall FitzGerald brought to the chairmanship of the then still troubled British Museum a great stability. He knew that the BM, its objects, keepers and curators, historic sense of purpose and responsibility were far greater than himself or any of us transients on the board. He knew too that in the director, Neil MacGregor, he had one of the great museum leaders of our time. FitzGerald's sense of mission and purpose was to serve, to assist, to support the director; to advise and counsel him, make good the lacunae in the director's abilities and to shield the BM's independence from political or external predations. He invested the chairman's role with a sense of responsibility and an understanding that it was a personal privilege to support the British Museum for a few moments in its long history. There was nothing sentimental about Niall FitzGerald. A sense of distance was needed as well as a sense of involvement. He provided both. FitzGerald once observed that perhaps he and MacGregor got on so well because they were both Celts, both outsiders.

At English National Opera (ENO), John Baker offered an approach of apparent simplicity and common sense. He expected to know what was going on; he expected to be able to range freely in his understanding about the company; he expected that agreements with public funders once struck would be honoured. He insisted that the company was run efficiently. Often disappointed but rarely discouraged, Baker did not overstep the chairman's role but was not prepared to have it circumscribed by the executive. If he was disappointed in his expectations, he was not wrong to demand them. He offered and gave clarity and stability in a situation where both were usually in short supply. His manner was occasionally too dry for some, but there was no self-indulgence in his behaviour. The gap of outlook and temperament between him as Chairman and his General Directors would have been unbridgeable by anyone.

The worst chairman I ever served under was Marmaduke ('Duke') Hussey at the BBC. He was arrogant and ignorant in equal measure: arrogant about his supposed social position and abilities, ignorant of the complexities and purposes of a great broadcasting organization. He broke every rule in the governance rulebook. Hussey looked down on his chief executive, Director-General Michael Checkland, whose slight 'Brummie' accent and Methodist background he found hard to accept. He redoubled the crisis of leadership at the top by nominating a successor to the post of Director-General while Checkland was still in post. Hussey disliked what the BBC stood for, was hostile to the entire senior executive team, often stoked up antagonism between the Board of Governors and the executive. He was hard to brief, reluctant to learn, often slow in his grasp of major issues. Finally, he got a chief executive who shared his dislike of BBC values but whose radical instincts he failed to spot and came to regret. During his chairmanship, the BBC was riven, bitterly divided and driven in directions that never gained full internal consent. As a case study in how not to be a chairman, Hussey at the BBC must stand as a classic. His failure derives straight from his lack of humanity: he was a bully.

Others will judge my record as chair of three organizations: Wigmore Hall, University of the Arts London and Clore Leadership Programme. In a spirit of self-appraisal, I offer this. At all three organizations I had deep, close, regular, confidential, trusting relations with my chief executives: John Gilhooly, Nigel Carrington and Sue Hoyle. We were at one over the purposes, values and direction of each organization. They were enriching experiences, personally and professionally, deepened by the satisfaction of overseeing three organizations which grew significantly under great executive leadership. I was most satisfied with the reshaping of the UAL Court of Governors broadening its composition of women and ethnic diversity.

If I occasionally lacked control over the Wigmore Hall board in a way that caused difficulties for the director, John Gilhooly, it never threatened our mutual trust or pushed the Hall's strategy off-track. If I sometimes seemed to undermine Sue Hoyle's strategies for change at Clore Leadership Programme, we never lost momentum or personal confidence in one another. At University of the Arts London, Vice-Chancellor Nigel Carrington knew exactly how to keep my enthusiasms and impatience in check without losing sight of the aims we shared and results that we achieved.

Apart from Dame Vivien Duffield at the Clore Leadership Programme, I witnessed two instances of extraordinary personal involvement in a project. The European Union Youth Orchestra (EUYO) was the sole creation of a wife-and-husband team, Joy and Lionel Bryer. This American/South African duo was fired with belief in European unity and the way that music among Europe's youth could serve its ideals. For 40 years, Joy Bryer was Director and nagged and persuaded politicians in every country in the European project as it evolved to support this example of the common goal in action. She was tireless, irresistible in her determination and unshakeable in her beliefs. The EUYO became a living demonstration of the European dream in practice and created a body of musicians who peopled the ranks of Europe's greatest orchestras. The Bryers' original idea was daring but a good one: they tested it in reality, forged it through hard-won success. No committee or consultancy could ever have dared to conceive, create or sustain it. The risks would have been judged too great, the chances of success too remote, the ambition too high. So much for the wisdom of calculation; it understands so little of the power of the human personality.

Not the least of Joy Bryer's achievements was to recognize that after almost 40 years as Director, she had to step aside. She passed on the leadership to two people who she knew and trusted: Ian Stoutzker, long-time supporter of the London Symphony Orchestra (LSO), and myself, a long-time family friend. We agreed to become co-chairmen. No headhunting took place, no governance succession procedures. Joy made the choice of her successors personal. When an organization has the stamp of an individual on it, when the founder's personality is so utterly embedded, when that personality has delivered almost half a century of achievement, the minutiae of formal governance take second place. Besides, she was best placed to understand how the future needs of the EUYO could be best met.

Over the succeeding four years, Ian Stoutzker and I Europeanized the
board, formalized its procedures and shaped the governance needed by an
entity that was looking to a settled future. The transition from the personal,
visionary and inspirational origins to the more formal needs of the next
state of the EUYO's existence was necessary and right. Without Joy Bryer's
original, personal vision, without 40 years of her determination, there
would have been nothing to build on.

My other close experience of visionary initiation came from Rory
Stewart and his Turquoise Mountain Foundation. Shortly after his epic
winter walk through Afghanistan from Herat to Kabul in 2002, a journey
in which he almost perished, he undertook the restoration of the last
remaining historic quarter of Kabul, the district of Murat Khane. It should
have been dismissed as a hopeless project since it was an area of collapsed
mud brick houses, jumbled, shattered wooden screens, with its former
courtyards piled six feet deep with years of accumulated urban rubbish,
densely compacted with a generation of plastic bags. To remove decades
of detritus alone would have been a singular achievement in itself. Only
then could the renovation of several score mud brick and wood buildings
become a possibility. That is its own extraordinary story.

From the very beginning, as Stewart gathered support for the project
from national, international and private funders, he clearly had to set up
credible and acceptable governance. They required it; he needed it. This
was no time for an organized search for trustees. Rory had no time for
that. Instead he did the common sense and practical thing: he turned to
his friends and contacts. He knew them, knew what they did, what they
stood for – they would not let him down. A life-long family friend, I had
known Rory since his childhood and was happy to join the board and
back him in a daring, visionary, possibly impossible venture.

The fact that the first collection of Turquoise Mountain Trustees
was picked by Rory does not contradict the general practices of good

governance. Each trustee was a formidable professional with relevant skills. Each brought a questioning mind and searching eye to the project. The governance required at the start of such an unlikely undertaking could not be more different from the staid processes of an established organization. Besides, the activity the trustees supervised was 4,000 miles away from Edinburgh, the legal base. As Turquoise Mountain evolved, its governance had to become more international, professional, systematic and fully in line with governance requirements demanded by international donors. The supervision of a start-up working in a different continent creates considerable difficulties. Appropriate governance had to be personal, particular and specially engaged. The fact that TMF's governance evolved as the institution itself changed wholly validated the necessarily less formal way in which it started. Besides, it was a human response to a singular act of personal, human imagination: governance should be a support for endeavour, not a straitjacket of restrictions.

By contrast, the practices of governance are simply ignored or not understood in some institutions. I experienced both such: one an academic body, Wolfson College, Cambridge, the other professional, the Royal Institute of British Architects (RIBA).

At Wolfson College, power officially resided in a Council of elected College Fellows. Real power lay in a small clique of fellows who saw themselves as the arbiters of such matters as they thought were important. In some respects they saw themselves as the true college – the main body of fellows was largely ignored and in truth took little interest in the doings of Council, which they regarded as a distraction from their scholarship. True power lay with the bursar, who controlled the finances. De facto, he was the nearest thing to a chief executive in the College structure. If his priority was to keep most real decisions away from the council, his greater interest seemed to be to challenge the President of the College – myself – from initiating any policies or taking any decisions.

All the ingredients for a breakdown in governance existed. The chairman (College President) and chief executive (Bursar) were badly matched and temperamentally poles apart. The president had been elected because the College felt flattered by the thought of appointing a television figure as its head. The president accepted the appointment because his vanity was flattered by heading a Cambridge College. The president thought the College wanted to make something of itself whereas the College merely wanted to continue to exist as a static community. The bursar accused the president of not understanding the nature of authority in a college. The president saw the bursar as arrogating that authority to himself through his control of finances. Members of College Council never challenged the bursar, offering minimal scrutiny and minimal time in attending to college business.

With warring leaders at the top, an unchallenged chief executive, an indifferent and inattentive governing body, every element of bad governance practice was in place. Some might argue that an academic college exists to 'be' not in order to 'do'. Looked at from a governance viewpoint, any institution needs some appropriate simulacrum of governance to exist in its own terms, whatever they are. Wolfson lacked this and was a miserable, unsuccessful place as a result. I would not have put it like this at the time but any institution must attempt serious governance. It need be neither cumbersome nor intrusive but should exist in some recognized and accepted form. The College declined to even make a pretence of the attempt. My way out was to resign at 48 hours' notice with a speed that the College thought was impossible. But my Wolfson time convinced me that a place without governance was no place to be part of.

The Royal Institute of British Architects (RIBA), unlike Wolfson College, Cambridge, has governance aplenty. An elected president on a two-year term, an elected executive board, a council of 60 elected architects representing the membership, an appointed chief executive running a large administration ... what could go wrong? Everything, because at RIBA, the governance was precisely upside down. The council of elected members reigned supreme; no president had the time, authority or the inclination to challenge or reform; the chief executive was treated as a lower-scale lackey reluctant to challenge the 'supreme' body; the administration, filled with competent officers, were treated like servants whose recommendations were seldom given full weight.

The usual justification for this bizarre arrangement was that 'RIBA is a members' organization'. This was held to justify placing members at the very summit of the policy and decision-making summit. The result was disastrous. It ignored that no organization can be led by a body of 60 people; it gave members of the council an overweening sense of personal importance and assumed authority. It shackled the role of the president (as it was intended to do); it emasculated the chief executive (also as intended); it obstructed the necessary creative interaction between president and chief executive; it undermined the professional effectiveness of well-qualified administrators. It undoubtedly satisfied the colossal vanity of some of those elected to the council, but that should have been seen as meagre justification for a governance structure as perverse as it was ineffective.

In a memo I wrote in December 2016 as I ended a brief connection with RIBA, I asked: 'Is a governance system where the President only presides, the Chief Executive carries out instructions and the staff feel tied a good one?' I added for good measure: 'Is the Council just a forum for indulging members' personal whims?' I never received an answer.

Above all, placing the beneficiaries of an institution in control of its affairs violates a founding principle of governance given me by my great American guru, Kenneth Dayton. He insisted that those with a direct interest in an institution should not as a matter of law and propriety be involved in supervising its affairs. The ruling principle of good governance must be that effective supervision and scrutiny can only come from those without a material interest in the results. RIBA's governance regime ignored this in the misguided name of being a 'members' organization'.

Perhaps the difficulties of providing good governance and the all-too-human failings that emerge can be traced to the very vagueness of the areas in which it operates and the necessary imprecision. One way of looking at the difficulty is through the prism of four antitheses: responsibility and power, accountability and interference, support and complacency, compliance and speculation.

A board has the responsibility to secure the activity of the organization by ensuring its financial, operational and legal viability. The power it has to do so is extremely limited, ranging from rejecting the executives' proposals to dismissing the chief executive. These are extreme sanctions with very little in between. The gap between the absoluteness of the responsibility and the extremity of any method of exercising it may be at the heart of the problem.

A board demands and expects accountability for the executives' policies and actions. If those expectations of accountability are too onerous, what is to stop them from turning into interference in executive business, intrusion into areas which should lie beyond board questioning?

A board should support the institution that it represents, should be a public cheerleader for its existence, its interests and its cause. Is there a risk that such support, however well-intentioned, becomes uncritical, ignores failings in the leaders and in the organization and topples over into being uncritical? Might the resulting complacency undermine the operation of accountability and the principle of responsibility? Yet, if a board will not speak up for the organization, why should anybody else?

Finally, boards must ensure the organization complies with its myriad legal obligations. If compliance appears the be-all and end-all of board activity, what happens to thought, speculation, adventure, imagination?

No sure, simple answers exist. Every board, each board member, has to trace their way through the large undefined spaces that exist within the boundaries of these antitheses: responsibility and power, accountability and interference, support and complacency, compliance and speculation. Every board will chart a different path through or across them. Some flounder and get lost in the attempt, some will baulk at the effort, others find them too difficult. All have an obligation to try or they should not be involved in governance. That is why it is such a human, undefinable, challenging but often rewarding cause to be involved in.

Despite the manuals, the nostrums, the theories, the prescriptions, governance is about the uncertain, the unpredictable but above all, the human. There is no single model that works, no assured formula for success, no guarantee of satisfaction, personal or professional.

At the 'Governance Now' conference on 13 November 2018, I decided to compress my thoughts into six provocative statements. This is how they turned out:

1   All board members are equal.

2   There are no stupid questions.

3   Boards should not be treated like mushrooms – kept in the dark and fed horse manure.

4   'What's in it for me?' Nothing except the occasional free ticket or board dinner.

5   'You don't run the organization.' That's for the executive.

6   'You'll always hear it from me first.' What a chair says to their chief executive.

Observing these points won't solve every governance difficulty. They might just make life on board much more satisfying.

9

Fifty Things They Say about Governance

How to Join a Board

'When you are asked to join a board, approach it like a job. What is the company? What are its values? What has it done? Work through the vanity reaction, the privilege reaction. Where is my value added?'

Farooq Chaudhry, Executive Director, Akram Khan Company

'I have a theory that if somebody asked me to go on a board, what I would like is to say "Thank you very much but I would like to spend a year or two as an observer seeing if I understand the business enough to go on the board." But I know they would say "No".'

Sir David Scholey, Chairman, National Portrait Gallery

'These are grand, great institutions, which have to be preserved. You step up as your way of serving the nation. We all gave our time, you weren't paid, but it was a wonderful experience to become part and parcel of the Museum.'

Baroness Kennedy of the Shaws, Trustee, British Museum

'What advice would I give to a board newcomer? Know the board, get the best and give the best; if you have the time do it, you will learn an awful lot. Remember, you and me, we are part of a circus, we are passed on from one board to another like a rugby ball!'

Tom Phillips, artist, Royal Academician, Trustee, British Museum

'Most of the things that go wrong with organizations come from governance. We tend to appoint boards in our own image.'

Nichola Johnson, Director,
Museum Leadership Course, University of East Anglia

How to Behave on a Board

'Two qualities emerge from all my board experience: you need independence of mind and spirit and intellectual rigour. Also, readiness to be unpopular. Too many boards lack backbone.'

Lord Chandos, Board Member, English National Opera

'Knowledge needs to be accountable. After a Board, ask yourself what questions should I have asked? Did I press for good answers? Facts do not speak for themselves, they need interrogation.'

Stephen Salyer, President, Public Radio International, Minneapolis

'Don't take on too many boards. Realize how limited is the clout that you will have. On some you will be just window dressing, on some you can make a difference. Have a feeling for which is which.'

Lord Rees, Trustee, British Museum

'I think you have to put your back into it. You've got to spend enough time with the people, going to the events and chatting, and not just visiting the new gallery but going into the basement and the stores. To understand enough of what's going on so that you can ask the right questions.'

Sir David Norgrove, Trustee, British Museum

'Don't expect the Board to actually develop the strategy. It's all very well, but a lot of rubbish is spoken about strategy.'

David Lindsell, Chair, Audit Committee, British Museum

'So many chief executives say it would be wonderful if you could get board members to see the organization's work, not just attend first nights. Surely the pleasure of the job is actually seeing the work, isn't it?'

Prue Skene, governance consultant

'I still ask questions unencumbered by business or political experience. I always try to be as much "me" as possible. I think, "What would Grayson say at this point?" But when people say in a discussion, "As Grayson said earlier," I am very pleased. After all, I'm just the artist on the Board!'

Grayson Perry, artist, Chancellor, University of the Arts London

'The top five risks are so obvious: the government support mechanism, recruitment of students and so on. We really want to know about our reputational risk elsewhere. Focussing on risk independently of the business is nuts. It is just the other side of opportunity. I find the "risk-business" very off-putting.'

David Lindsell, Chair, Audit Committee,
University of the Arts London

'If people are going to be an effective governor of a university they have to give quite a lot of time. An awayday is not enough. Being involved in a committee is almost essential if you are going to be effective. If people didn't join just because it was something to add to their CV but joined because they had some expertise to bring that would make them a better governor.'

Lorraine Baldry, Governor, University of the Arts London

'One of my board members saw his role as to push back rather than to improve things. He wanted to flex his muscles, to have the upper hand. I did not find this useful behaviour.'

Stephen Salyer, President, Public Radio International, Minneapolis

'All organizations find it hard to devise a genuine and rigorous strategy. There are three basic questions: "What is the situation the organization faces?", "How much money does it have?", "What are the solutions you can achieve within the budget?" Instead we produced a "mission statement" but it was gibberish.'

Sir Rodric Braithwaite, Board Member, English National Opera

'Do people know one another on a board? Do they know what they are doing? What is the time span of a meeting? Does everyone have the chance to speak? Who is talking too much? Where are we in the discussion? When should we return to the subject?'

Sandy Nairne, Director, National Portrait Gallery

'Strategy and mission in an opera house are very difficult. I always say, "Measure it if you want to manage it." Others say, "In the arts so many things can't be measured." I say, "You need to create proxies to measure what you do."'

Sir Anthony Cleaver, Board Member, English National Opera

'I once sat on a board where you wondered at the end of each meeting what the organization was for. The Board didn't know where it fitted in. There was no sense that it was helping to set a direction or hold the organization to account.'

Lord Smith of Finsbury, Director, Clore Leadership Programme

'Some of them were on too many boards to focus on the strategy. I made it a rule to talk directly to anyone who seemed to have an issue within 24 hours of the board meeting to clear up misunderstandings. This seemed to work pretty well – I think that most of them would rather not have had one of those phone calls with me than endure one!'

Russell Willis Taylor, Executive Director, English National Opera

'The two essential qualities of a successful investment banker are an equal balance between ambition and anxiety. I always wanted the feeling on a board that people were not only responsible for what they knew about, but also for what they did not know about.'

Sir David Scholey, Chairman, National Portrait Gallery

Chairman and Chief Executive

'If there is an inherent tension between the Chair and the Chief executive, you're not going to share. If you don't share, there isn't the necessary transparency. If you don't have transparency, you don't have trust.'

Sir Nigel Carrington, Vice-Chancellor,
University of the Arts London

'I always used to say to my chief executive, "I don't want to be surprised!" I never wanted them to come and say, "Chairman, we've had a terrific success, here's a surprise!" I never want to be surprised because that would mean you're going to keep me au fait with what you think I need to know. Also, I tried to give people the feeling that I would probably find out.'

Sir David Scholey, Chairman, National Portrait Gallery

'The Chair should focus Board support for the CEO, give advice that is friendly but critical. There should be no misalignment about contact, meetings or papers. The CEO can get on with the job, but always tell the Chair first. Once a year, "Let's have dinner en famille".'

Sandy Nairne, Director, National Portrait Gallery

'The most successful outfits are where the Chairman and Chief Executive really forge a good relationship. If it's not working, it will have repercussions down through the organization. If you're going to create the idea that we are in this together, we're going to make it work, we're going to have fun, we're going to make it wonderful, we're going to be proud of what we have achieved, that's the thing!'

Baroness Kennedy of the Shaws, Trustee, British Museum

'It's always the case that the Chair is your closest confidant as chief executive but also the person who ultimately can fire you. The relationship is one of private debate, the best debate you can have to sort things out between board meetings. The Chair should be thinking how is the totality of the museum working, is it moving forward, is it moving according to its strategy? Chairs manage the Board, the executive manages the management.'

Lord Browne of Madingley, Trustee, British Museum

'A very good friend said this to me about the way I was chairing a board: "Could we discuss things to which you don't know the answer before we start?" I was a very different chairman after that'.

Sir David Scholey, Chairman, National Portrait Gallery

'Every director is going to feel lonely. It's a struggle. I had this absolutely confidential person as chair, with great wisdom and experience, that really helped me enormously. The board on any museum is an enormous resource to be used in providing expertise in all kinds of areas that cannot be found either in academic staff or even in the business world.'

Neil MacGregor, Director, British Museum

'I like to see progress in manageable bites and not get bogged down in something which is too ambitious and then runs into problems. Then I believe in taking people with me at every stage. You don't just say we're going to do this. Therefore, there's consensual support for the direction the place is going.'

Michael Cassidy, Chairman,
Barbican Centre Committee, City of London Corporation

'I have now refused to do any "non-exec" work except arts and charity. You get files of stuff from audit and risk committees. You haven't got much power or influence over them. They say you will be severely responsible if something goes wrong. What's the point? Some people build careers on it. Chairs have a responsibility to segment the boring bits and use "non-execs" properly for strategic contribution.'

David Kershaw, Chair, M&C Saatchi

'Your Money or Your Art?'

'It is the character of the people in the arts world. They don't like financial discipline. It is thought to be non-artistic to be interested in money. Boards should be tougher in appointing general directors who are attuned to financial discipline, not artistic innovation.'

Bob Boas, Board Member, English National Opera

'My experience from working with arts leaders is that they are absolutely obsessed with their vision of how the company should be that in varying degrees they are not capable of delivering. They simply do not put in the hard grind of translating ideas into efficient systems which are fundamental parts of management.'

Sir John Baker, Chairman, English National Opera

'My Trustees did not recognize that the Museum was a business organization but also an intellectual organization. Arts organizations are not businesses.'

Malcolm Rogers, Director, Museum of Fine Arts, Boston

'Profit never hurt an arts company. People who say that have a comic-book picture of capitalism and business. Even sensible journalists think that unless you are artistically led, by definition, you have nothing to contribute.'

Sir John Baker, Chairman, English National Opera

'With something like a museum it's far more complex than a business, size for size. If the turnover of the British Museum is, say, £50 million, it is probably 20 times more complex than a £50 million business.'

Lord Browne of Madingley, Trustee, British Museum

'British board activity is a million miles away from that of the United States over giving. Any board member must have two of the four "Ws" – "wealth, work, wisdom and wow"!'

Theresa Lloyd, development consultant

'In the United States, trustees ask, "Am I giving appropriately?"'

Malcolm Rogers, Director, Museum of Fine Arts, Boston

'If arts organizations are to continue to thrive in the United Kingdom, they are going to have to get better at defining board responsibilities. This will have to include defining giving expectations. In London, some trustees were indignant at being asked for financial support.'

Sir Clive Gillinson, Director, Carnegie Hall, New York

'The Wigmore Hall board is not a fundraising board, it was never meant to be. It is an administrative board, it has been brilliant on compliance without letting governance get in the way. I've learned a lot about how to use governance without stifling your chief executive and senior management team.'

John Gilhooly, Director, Wigmore Hall

'The CEO should not be a prima donna and that's a difficulty. In a business you have the numbers that are fairly irrefutable as measurements of success. On an arts board you don't have that. You're trying to measure the quality of something like music and art and what is valid novelty and what is not. I think they're more difficult than a corporate board.'

Lord Broers, Trustee, British Museum

'Politics – Keep Them at Arm's Length'

'That's one of the things trustee boards in Britain don't adequately internalize: what it means to be funded by Government and answerable to Parliament. You're not part of Government policy, you're answerable to Parliament. As Accounting Officer, I don't answer to the Minister, I answer to Parliament. That is a huge distinction.'

Neil MacGregor, Director, British Museum

'Museum chairmen were discussing objectives with ministers and officials. I said, "In more than 37 years in business, if I got an entire company to accept, buy into and act towards three to four objectives, we were doing very well. You can't have more than six." I thought the Minister looked a bit pale. Later, a civil servant told me, "We just agreed 48 departmental objectives this morning"!'

Niall FitzGerald, Chairman, British Museum

'I've seen Arts Council appointments made where manifestly brilliant people have been turned down for no reason at all and somebody completely unqualified has been put in by the Minister. Either because he's a chum or because he exemplifies some political virtue which may or may not be relevant to the institution. They make appointments on the basis of a hierarchy of patronage, which is a disaster.'

Dame Liz Forgan, Trustee, British Museum

'I once had to say to a minister: "What you probably don't fully understand, there's nothing that you can do to me that worries me. There's nothing you can give me that I want. So please don't assume you have any sway over me which would counteract my strong view about my responsibility to maintain the independence of the institution".'

Niall FitzGerald, Chairman, British Museum

The Funny Side

'Neil MacGregor and I would have this joke. We would come into our offices for years, promulgating all this thing about "The Museum of the World for the World" and all that rhetoric. Then one day, we would leave and all the curators would look at one another and say, "Ah, now they've gone" and carry on as normal and nothing would change.'

Dawn Austwick, Deputy Director, British Museum

'The Trustees went on an awayday to Suffolk in a mini-coach. We stopped at a Happy Eater on the A13. Out they all got, the American Ambassador, Sir Joe Hotung and the Duke of Gloucester. The Duke said, "I've never been in one of these!" The host said, "We don't serve parties!" One trustee said, "We only want a cup of tea!" The host said, "Alright then." It was absolutely glorious, it was the British Museum Trustees go on holiday, it was just hilarious.'

Dawn Austwick, Deputy Director, British Museum

'The Board never discussed why we never put new productions "out to tender". It was like picking your nose on *Newsnight*!'

Charles Alexander, Board Member, English National Opera

'A former Vice-Chancellor of Oxford University was once asked if being Vice-Chancellor was a "full-time occupation". He replied, "No, it is a full-time pre-occupation"!'

Sir Keith Thomas, Trustee, British Museum

'I'm a great believer that the value of a mistake is that it is a unique learning opportunity. So let's learn from it so that we do not repeat it and that we get it better the next time round.'

Niall FitzGerald, Chairman, British Museum

Life Goes On

'We develop patterns, they play to our strengths. But a little bit of disruption can be a good thing.'

Farooq Chaudhry, Executive Director, Akram Khan Company

'There's a virtuous circle. As the reputation of the organization builds, the kind of people you can recruit goes up. People want to be part of it, that's a piece of human nature that is still there. But you must treat them well and mustn't let them down.'

Stephen Barter, Vice-Chair, University of the Arts London

SOURCES

1. The National Portrait Gallery: The Trustees' Rebellion (1988–2000)

NPG Board Minutes, 1989–2000.
NPG Annual Reports, 1989–2000.
Claire Tomalin letter to author.
Author's letter to Professor Owen Chadwick, 24 September 1993.
Strong, Roy (2017), *Splendours and Miseries: The Roy Strong Diaries, 1967–87*, London, Weidenfeld & Nicolson.
Press reports.
Thanks to Pim Baxter, Deputy Director, National Portrait Gallery (NPG); Bryony Millan, Librarian, NPG.

2. Taking Governance Seriously: The American Way (1991–1999)

Patty Johnson kindly made available an unofficial chronology of milestones in APR/PRI business 1991–98.
Arning, Bill, Baily Wieler, Mary (February 2019), 'Is the US Trustee System Good for Museums?', *Apollo* magazine.
Dayton, Kenneth N. (1987), 'Governance is Governance', independent sector.
'Leading with Intent 2017', Board Source survey.

3. English National Opera: Board Without Power (1994–2004)

Lord Harewood in a letter to author, 2 February 1994.
Morrison, Richard, 'Final Curtain for Opera at Coliseum', *The Times*, 10 May 1996.
Gilbert, Susie (2009), *Opera for Everybody: The Story of English National Opera*, London, Faber & Faber.
English National Opera Board Book.
General press articles.
Communication with Russell Willis Taylor, Sir Vernon Ellis.

4. The British Museum: 'A Most August and Ancient Board' (2000–09)

British Museum, Board Minutes, May 1999 to November 2008.
British Museum Annual Reports, 2000 to 2009.
Tom Phillips, RA (2005), *Merry Meetings*, London, D3 Editions.
Whittam Smith, Andreas, 'Is the British Museum Losing its Marbles?' *Independent*,
    18 November 1996.
Tusa, John, 'Farewell to Sir Keith Thomas' speech, 26 February 2008.
Tusa, John, 'Farewell to the British Museum' speech, 26 March 2009.
Written communications from David Lindsell, David Norgrove, Keith Thomas and
    Martin Rees.

5. The Wigmore Years: Chairmanship is Harder Than You Think (1999–2011)

Macrae, Julia (ed.), 'The Score – Wigmore Hall – 110 Years'.
Macrae, Julia (ed.), 'Wigmore Hall – 1901–2001: A Celebration'.
Ehrlich, Cyril, 'The First Hundred Years'.
Macrae, Julia (ed.), 'The Score' – 2002, 2003, 2004, 2005, 2006, 2007, 2008, 2009.

6. University of the Arts London (UAL): Unity from Diversity (2007–13)

Court of Governors' Minutes, July 2007–May 2013.
University of the Arts London (UAL) Annual Report and Financial Statements,
    2010–12.
'University Governance in a New Age of Regulation', HEPI Report No. 119, August 2019.
Tusa, John (2018), *Making a Noise: Getting it Right, Getting it Wrong in Life, the Arts
    and Broadcasting*, Chapter 13, London, Weidenfeld & Nicolson.

7. Clore Leadership Programme (CLP): Shaping an Idea – Governance in a 'Start-up' (2008–2014)

John Holden and Robert Hewison, 'Cultural Leadership – the Clore Leadership
    Programme Task Force Final Report', December 2002, Clore Duffield Foundation.

INDEX